THE CHURCH AT WORSHIP: CASE STUDIES FROM CHRISTIAN HISTORY

Series Editors: LESTER RUTH, CARRIE STEENWYK, JOHN D. WITVLIET

Published

Walking Where Jesus Walked: Worship in Fourth-Century Jerusalem
    Lester Ruth, Carrie Steenwyk, John D. Witvliet

Forthcoming

Tasting Heaven on Earth: Worship in Sixth-Century Constantinople
    Walter D. Ray

Following Jesus Only: Worship at a Black Holiness Church,
Early Twentieth Century
    Lester Ruth

Loving God Intimately: Worship with John Wimber
at Anaheim Vineyard Fellowship
    Andy Park, Lester Ruth, and Cindy Rethmeier

Walking Where

Jesus Walked

Worship in Fourth-Century Jerusalem

Lester Ruth

Carrie Steenwyk

John D. Witvliet

William B. Eerdmans Publishing Company
Grand Rapids, Michigan / Cambridge, U.K.

Published 2010 by Wm. B. Eerdmans Publishing Co.
2140 Oak Industrial Drive N.E., Grand Rapids, Michigan 49505 /
P.O. Box 163, Cambridge CB3 9PU U.K.

Printed in the United States of America

14 13   7 6 5 4 3 2

Library of Congress Cataloging-in-Publication Data

Ruth, Lester, 1959-
  Walking where Jesus walked : worship in fourth-century Jerusalem / Lester Ruth.
    p.   cm.   — (The church at worship)
  Includes bibliographical references (p.   ) index.
  ISBN 978-0-8028-6476-5 (pbk. : alk. paper)
  1. Public worship — Jerusalem — History — Textbooks.
  2. Jerusalem — Church history — Textbooks. 3. Liturgies, Early Christian — Textbooks.
  4. Church history — Primitive and early church, ca. 30–600 — Textbooks.   I. Title.
  BV185.R87   2010
  264.00933 — dc22

                                  2010029164

www.eerdmans.com

Contents

Series Introduction

The Church at Worship offers user-friendly documentary case studies in the history of Christian worship. The series features a wide variety of examples, both prominent and obscure, from a range of continents, centuries, and Christian traditions. Whereas many historical studies of worship survey developments over time, offering readers a changing panoramic view like that offered out of an airplane window, each volume in *The Church at Worship* zooms in close to the surface, lingering over worship practices in a single time and place and allowing readers to sense the texture of specific worship practices in unique Christian communities. To complement books that study "the forest" of liturgical history, these volumes study "trees in the forest."

Each volume opens by orienting readers to the larger contexts of each example through a map, a timeline of events, and a summary of significant aspects of worship in the relevant time period and region. This section also includes any necessary cautions for the study of the particular case, as well as significant themes or practices to watch for while reading.

Each volume continues by focusing on the practices of worship in the specific case. This section begins with an introduction that explains the nature of participation in worship for ordinary worshipers. Many studies of worship have focused almost exclusively on what clergy do, say, and think. In contrast, insofar as historical sources allow it, this series focuses on the nature of participation of the entire community.

Each volume next presents an anthology of primary sources, presenting material according to the following categories: people and artifacts, worship setting and space, descriptions of worship, orders of worship and texts, sermons, polity documents, and theology-of-worship documents. Each source is introduced briefly and is accompanied by a series of explanatory notes. Inclusion of these primary sources allows readers to have direct access to the primary material that historians draw upon for their summary descriptions and comparisons of practices. These sources are presented in ways that honor both academic rigor and accessibility. Our aim is to provide the best English editions of the resources possible, along with a complete set of citations that allow researchers to find quickly the best scholarly editions. At the same time, the introductory comments, explanatory sidebars, detailed glossaries, and devotional and small-group study questions make these volumes helpful not only for scholars and students but also for congregational study groups and a variety of other interested readers.

The presentation of sources attempts, insofar as it is possible, to take into account multiple disciplines of study related to worship. Worship is inevitably a multi-sensory experience, shaped by the sounds of words and music, the sight of symbols and spaces, the taste of bread and wine, and the fragrance of particular places and objects. Worship is also shaped by a variety of sources that never appear in the event itself: scriptural commands, theological treatises, and church polity rules or guidelines. In order to help readers sense this complex interplay, the volumes in this series provide a wide variety of texts and images. We particularly hope that this approach helps students of the history of preaching, architecture, and music, among others, to more deeply understand how their interests intersect with other disciplines.

Each volume concludes with suggestions for devotional use, study questions for congregational study groups, notes for students working in a variety of complementary disciplines, a glossary, suggestions for further study, works cited, and an index.

Students of Christian worship, church history, religious studies, and social or cultural history might use these case studies to complement the bird's-eye view offered by traditional textbook surveys.

Students in more specialized disciplines — including both liberal arts humanities (e.g., architectural or music history) and the subdisciplines of practical theology (e.g., evangelism, preaching, education, and pastoral care) — may use these volumes to discern how their own topic of interest interacts with worship practices. Liturgical music, church architecture, and preaching, for example, cannot be fully understood apart from a larger context of related practices.

This series is also written for congregational study groups, adult education classes, and personal study. It may be unconventional in some contexts to plan a congregational study group around original historical documents. But there is much to commend this approach. A reflective encounter with the texture of local practices in other times and places can be a profound act of discipleship. In the words of Andrew Walls, "Never before has the Church looked so much like the great multitude whom no one can number out of every nation and tribe and people and tongue. Never before, therefore, has there been so much potentiality for mutual enrichment and self-criticism, as God causes yet more light and truth to break forth from his word."[1]

This enrichment and self-criticism happens, in part, by comparing and contrasting the practices of another community with our own. As Rowan Williams explains, "Good history makes us think again about the definition of things we thought we understood pretty well, because it engages not just with what is familiar but with what is strange. It recognizes that 'the past is a foreign country' as well as being *our* past."[2] This is possible, in part, because of a theological conviction. As Williams points out, ". . . there is a sameness in the work of God. . . . We are not the first to walk this way; run your hand down the wood and the grain is

1. Andrew Walls, *The Missionary Movement in Christian History: Studies in the Transmission of Faith* (Maryknoll, N.Y.: Orbis Books, 1996), p. 15.
2. Rowan Williams, *Why Study the Past? The Quest for the Historical Church* (Grand Rapids: Wm. B. Eerdmans, 2005), p. 1.

still the same."[3] This approach turns on its head the minimalist perspective that "those who cannot remember the past are condemned to repeat it."[4] That oft-repeated truism implies that the goal of studying history is merely to avoid its mistakes. A more robust Christian sensibility is built around the conviction that the past is not just a comedy of errors but the arena in which God has acted graciously.

We pray that as you linger over this and other case studies in this series, you will be challenged and blessed through your encounter with one small part of the very large family of God. Near the end of his magisterial volume *A Secular Age,* Charles Taylor concludes, "None of us could ever grasp alone everything that is involved in our alienation from God and his action to bring us back. But there are a great many of us, scattered through history, who have had some powerful sense of some facet of this drama. Together we can live it more fully than any one of us could alone." What might this mean? For Taylor it means this: "Instead of reaching immediately for the weapons of polemic, we might better listen for a voice which we could never have assumed ourselves, whose tone might have been forever unknown to us if we hadn't *strained to understand it. . . .*"[5] We hope and pray that readers, eager to learn from worship communities across time and space, will indeed strain to understand what they find in these studies.

LESTER RUTH
Asbury Theological Seminary
The Robert E. Webber Institute for Worship Studies

CARRIE STEENWYK
Calvin Institute of Christian Worship
Calvin College and Calvin Theological Seminary

JOHN D. WITVLIET
Calvin Institute of Christian Worship
Calvin College and Calvin Theological Seminary

3. Williams, *Why Study the Past?* p. 29.
4. George Santayana, *The Life of Reason* (New York: Scribner's, 1905), p. 284.
5. Charles Taylor, *A Secular Age* (Cambridge: Harvard University Press, 2007), p. 754.

Suggestions for Complementary Reading

For students of Christian worship wanting to survey the broader landscape, we recommend using the examples of these volumes alongside other books such as Geoffrey Wainwright and Karen B. Westerfield Tucker's *Oxford History of Christian Worship* (Oxford University Press, 2005); Gail Ramshaw's *Christian Worship: 100,000 Sundays of Symbols and Rituals* (Fortress Press, 2009); Frank C. Senn's *The People's Work: A Social History of the Liturgy* (Fortress Press, 2006) and *Christian Liturgy: Catholic and Evangelical* (Fortress Press, 1997); and James F. White's *Introduction to Christian Worship* (Abingdon Press, 2001), *A Brief History of Christian Worship* (Abingdon Press, 1993), and *Protestant Worship* (Westminster John Knox Press, 2006).

For those studying church history, volumes from this series might accompany volumes such as Mark Noll's *Turning Points: Decisive Moments in the History of Christianity* (Baker Academic, 2001) and Justo Gonzalez's *Church History: An Essential Guide* (Abingdon Press, 1996) and *The Story of Christianity,* vols. 1-2 (HarperOne, 1984 and 1985).

Students of religious studies might read these volumes alongside Robert A. Segal's *The Blackwell Companion to the Study of Religion* (Wiley-Blackwell, 2008) and John R. Hinnell's *The Routledge Companion to the Study of Religion* (Routledge, 2005).

History of music classes might explore the case studies of this series with Paul Westermeyer's *Te Deum: The Church and Music* (Augsburg Fortress Publishers, 1998) or Andrew Wilson-Dickson's *The Story of Christian Music: From Gregorian Chant to Black Gospel* (Augsburg Fortress Publishers, 2003).

History of preaching students might study the contextual examples provided in this series along with Hughes Oliphant Old's volumes of *The Reading and Preaching of the Scriptures in the Worship of the Christian Church* (Eerdmans, 1998-2007) or O. C. Edwards's *A History of Preaching* (Abingdon Press, 2004).

Acknowledgments

We are grateful for the many people who helped make this volume possible:

to Calvin Brondyke, Matt Gritter, Kent Hendricks, Shelley Veenstra Hendricks, Courtney Hexham, Rachel Klompmaker, Jana Kelder Koh, Brenda Janssen Kuyper, Anneke Leunk, Asher Mains, Becky Boender Ochsner, Katie Roelofs, Katie Ritsema Roelofs, Eric Rottman, Annica Vander Linde, Bethany Meyer Vrieland, Tracie VerMerris Wiersma, Joanna Kooyenga Wigboldy, and Eric Zoodsma, whose work at the Calvin Institute of Christian Worship as student assistants has included hours of copying, scanning, typing, and other support for this volume;

to Harriet Cook, an administrative assistant at Asbury Theological Seminary, who provided valuable behind-the-scenes support;

to Jim Dodge, Michael Driscoll, Young Kim, and Martha Ann Kirk for their insights and critiques on earlier drafts of this material;

to students at Asbury Theological Seminary, Calvin College, Calvin Theological Seminary, and the Robert E. Webber Institute for Worship Studies, who inspired this series and whose class responses shaped this volume;

to teachers of liturgy, especially James F. White, in memoriam, for his love for teaching Christian worship through historical documents, through exploration of a wide diversity of Christian communities, and through exploration of worship from the perspective of all members of the worshiping community;

to Linda Borecki, Matthew Bowman, Joseph DeLeon, Isaac Gaff, Craig Ginn, Nancy Hale, Brian Hartley, Thomas Hutchison, Martha Ann Kirk, Kevin Livingston, Alan Rathe, Jonathan Riches, Sue Rozeboom, Linda Storm, and David Taylor, History of Worship Summer Seminar 2010 participants, for their helpful comments on the volume;

to Hugh Claycombe for the production of two historical re-creations of worship space included in this volume;

to John Lickwar for permission to include a photograph of the icon of St. Cyril of Jerusalem that he painted in the egg tempera medium;

to the Lilly Endowment for financial support;

and to Mary Hietbrink and Kevin van der Leek for assistance in the publication process.

PART ONE

LOCATING THE
WORSHIPING COMMUNITY

The Context of the Worshiping Community: Fourth-Century Jerusalem

Jerusalem is a holy site in three different religions: Judaism, Islam, and Christianity. And for all three it is an important site of pilgrimage. Faithful worshipers from all three want to go to the city because it is a kind of transparent place in which they can feel closer to the events which unfolded there. For Christians, the sensibility comes especially from the close association between the city and the dramatic scenes from the life and ministry of Jesus Christ. Who would not want to worship where Christ had stood, walked, bled, and rose? Not surprisingly, Christian desire to be a pilgrim in Jerusalem goes back to the early church.[1]

Doing so was not always easy in the early church, however, since, even in the initial New Testament period, the stability of the Jerusalem church got caught up in the growing tension between militant Jews and the Roman government.[2] Tensions so escalated that the Roman army laid siege to Jerusalem in A.D. 70. By late in the year, the Romans had defeated all of the city's resistance, demolishing the Temple and razing the city. Only a few buildings in the city's southwest outskirts survived. The Roman army established a camp to the north of this remnant. Ancient historians report that the Jewish Christians who had fled earlier, perhaps across the Jordan, now returned and settled in this surviving neighborhood. By the end of the first century, Jerusalem was mainly a military installation with a small suburb attached. Imagine a town in the boondocks tacked on to an army base. At this time there was no reason to make a pilgrimage to Jerusalem.

The next century brought even bigger changes. In the year 130 the emperor Hadrian visited the city. He decided that the site was in need of a dramatic renovation. He planned a new city, filled with the standard elements of Roman culture—including pagan temples. Adding insult to injury, Hadrian tried to compel the Jewish residents to give up their distinctive practices. The result was a guerrilla war eventually won by the Romans. When they were victorious, all Jews, including Jewish Christians, were banned from the city, and the emperor built his new city, whose Roman pagan character was clearly evident. For example, a new

---

1. For more information, see Peter Walker. "Pilgrimage in the Early Church," in *Explorations in a Christian Theology of Pilgrimage*, ed. Craig Bartholomew and Fred Hughes (Burlington: Ashgate, 2004).

2. For more information, see Karen Armstrong, *Jerusalem: One City, Three Faiths* (New York: Alfred A. Knopf, 1996), pp. 150-90, upon which the following account is dependent. See also Jerome Murphy-O'Connor, "Pre-Constantinian Christian Jerusalem," in *The Christian Heritage in the Holy Land,* ed. Anthony O'Mahony et al. (London: Scorpion Cavendish, 1995), pp. 13-21, and Oded Irshai, "From Oblivion to Fame: The History of the Palestinian Church (135-303 CE)," in *Christians and Christianity in the Holy Land: From the Origins to the Latin Kingdoms,* ed. Ora Limor and Guy G. Stroumsa (Turnhout, Belgium: Brepols, 2006), pp. 91-140.

temple to Venus (Aphrodite) was built on top of the area that Christians traditionally had associated with Jesus' crucifixion and resurrection. The Christians who formed the church that remained in the city in the second and third centuries appear to have been Gentile Christians who had moved there. Jerusalem's **bishop**[3], the highest order of ministry, did not hold a prominent position but was under the authority of another bishop with regional authority.

The fourth century marked an astonishing advancement for Jerusalem on the stage of worldwide Christianity.[4] The trigger was a Christian emperor, Constantine, whose rise and legalizing embrace of Christianity eventually—and dramatically—affected the nature of Jerusalem's church and its worship.

Under the sponsorship of Constantine, the city's bishop continually gained status among other bishops, and a new church, attached to major pilgrimage sites, developed. It appears likely that Macarius, Jerusalem's bishop in the early fourth century, discussed with the emperor a Christian building project for the city, because he eventually obtained the emperor's permission and financial support to demolish the Venus temple and try to uncover the tomb of Christ.[5] Work progressed quickly. (A visit in 326 by Helena, the emperor's mother and a devout Christian, helped spur progress.) Eventually, the site of Jesus' crucifixion was excavated and his tomb was discovered, to the great delight of the city's Christians. They thought they had even found Christ's cross! (Later, legend attributed the discovery to Helena.) The complex of buildings at the site honored all these discoveries by associating particular buildings with crucial moments in the life of Christ. Christian pilgrims now had reason to visit Jerusalem and something to see once they got there.

For Christians at the time, the buildings testified not only to historic events in the life of Christ but also to Christianity's resurgence against both Judaism and pagan religions. The complex at the site of Jesus' crucifixion and resurrection occupied a hill which towered over the desecrated, desolated Temple mount, the most sacred site in Judaism. And the buildings stood only because an emperor had agreed to demolish pagan temples.

In 335 the buildings at the crucifixion and resurrection sites were ready for consecration. Bishops from all the **dioceses** in the eastern provinces were summoned for the occasion. Clergy and laity, from Jerusalem and beyond, packed the site in wonder and amazement. They were only the first of many as pilgrims from across the Christian world flocked to the city.

The presence of all these pilgrims meant that services were held to satisfy their desire to worship at these special sites. Much in the services would seem familiar to them, since ser-

A diocese is a region or a group of churches over which a bishop has supervision.

---

3. Terms that are bold can be found in the Glossary.
4. Peter Walker, "Jerusalem and the Holy Land in the Fourth Century," in *The Christian Heritage in the Holy Land*, ed. Anthony O'Mahony et al., pp. 22-34.
5. A recent English translation of a letter from Macarius to the Armenian church discussing various worship matters in 335, at the time of the dedication of the new buildings, can be found in *Macarius of Jerusalem: Letter to the Armenians, A.D. 335*, trans. Abraham Terian (Crestwood, N.Y.: St. Vladimir's Seminary Press; New Rochelle, N.Y.: St. Nersess Armenian Seminary, 2008).

vices featuring multiple Scripture readings, a sermon, and the Lord's Supper were the main-stay of Christian worship at the time. These services, as elsewhere, were supplemented by additional services consisting largely of prayers. Baptism continued to be an important sign of identification with both Christ and the church. And, as was happening in other churches at the time, this worship was conducted on a large public scale with great ceremony and other elements to trigger a sense of awe among the worshipers. What was different about Jerusalem was the place, and how remembrance, Scripture, and symbol got connected intimately to the sites where Christ was born, suffered, and rose. The city found itself both exporting its practices to pilgrims who took them home and importing practices from these same visitors, which created a complex mix that would forever impact Christian worship.

After centuries of neglect and a return to its foundations, Jerusalem finally regained its position of significance by the late fourth century and became an important intersection for Christian worship practices from around the world.

Timeline

What was happening in the world?	What was happening in Christianity?
63 B.C.E.: Pompey claims Jerusalem for Rome.	
280: Constantine is born.	
285: The Roman Empire is divided into East and West.	303-4: Emperor Diocletian begins the Great Persecution.
	313: The "Edict" of Milan gives Christians full toleration.
312: Constantine leads his army to victory over rival Maxentius, attributing his success to Christ.	320: Constantine builds St. Peter's Basilica in Rome.
	323: Eusebius of Caesarea writes *Ecclesiastical History*.
324: Constantine reunites the Roman Empire and becomes sole emperor.	325: The Council of Nicea, the first general council of the church, affirms the deity of Christ, sets dates for celebration, gives norms on liturgy, and formulates the Nicene Creed.
Mid-300s: Constantine makes bishops a part of the political structure by giving them judicial power.	328: Athanasius of Alexandria becomes bishop in Egypt.
330: Constantinople is made the capital of the Roman Empire.	
335: The Roman Empire is divided between Constantine's sons.	
337: Constantine is baptized and dies.	
354-56: Germanic people invade Gaul.	354: Augustine of Hippo is born.
362: Emperor Julian "the Apostate" restores paganism.	
363: Julian dies.	
364-78: Valens, Roman Emperor of the East, sides with the Arians.	
ca. 360-70: The Huns invade Europe.	373: Athanasius of Alexandria dies.
	381: The First Council of Constantinople solidifies orthodox statements on the Persons of the Trinity; the Council affirms Cyril's orthodoxy and the validity of his consecration as bishop.
382: Roman Emperor Theodosius I declares heresy against Christianity as a capital crime.	
	386: Augustine converts to Christianity.
391: Theodosius I prohibits pagan worship.	ca. 395: Augustine becomes bishop of Hippo in North Africa.
395: After the death of Theodosius I, the empire is permanently divided into East and West.	397: Jerome translates the Bible into the Latin Vulgate.
	398: John Chrysostom, a priest from Antioch, becomes patriarch of Constantinople.
410: Rome is sacked.	431: The Council of Ephesus further refines the orthodox doctrine of Christ.
476: The Roman Empire (Western) falls.	

What was happening in the Jerusalem church?

ca. 62: James is stoned to death in Jerusalem at the instigation of the high priest.

70-73: Jews revolt against Rome. Early on the Roman army takes Jerusalem and burns the temple of Herod.

132-36: Jews are expelled from Jerusalem, which is renamed Aelia Capitolina, during the second great Jewish revolt (the Bar Kokhba Revolt) against Rome.

ca. 135: Hadrian tries to build a pagan temple to Jupiter on the Temple mount.

ca. 310: Cyril is born.

ca. 325: Helena, mother of Constantine, founds the Church of the Nativity in Bethlehem.

326: Building begins on the Church of the Holy Sepulcher.

335: The Council of Jerusalem reinstates Arius, although he is considered heretical by others.

335: The Martyrium (part of the Holy Sepulcher complex) is consecrated.

ca. 330-40s: Cyril is ordained as priest in Jerusalem.

ca. 336-48: The church at Sion, the original meeting-place of the post-Easter Christian community, is built.

mid-300s: Anastasis is likely built.

ca. 350: Cyril becomes bishop of Jerusalem.

357: Acacius, bishop of Caesarea, deposes Cyril, who goes into exile.

359: The Council of Seleucia, to which Cyril had appealed, reinstates Cyril and deposes Acacius.

360: Acacius persuades the Eastern emperor Constantius to reinstate him and depose Cyril.

361: Constantius dies, and Julian recalls all banished bishops.

363: The Jews attempt to rebuild on the Temple mount with encouragement from pagan emperor Julian.

367: Valens, the new Eastern emperor, reactivates sentences imposed by Constantius; Cyril is banished a third time.

378: Gratian, successor to Valens, recalls exiled bishops.

381-84: Egeria takes her pilgrimage.

ca. 380-90s: A church is built at the **Imbomon** (site on the Mount of Olives outside Jerusalem where Jesus was thought to have ascended to heaven).

386 or 387: Cyril dies.

Liturgical Landscape

What liturgical worlds surrounded Jerusalem in the late fourth century? If a Jerusalem worshiper looked around, what might he or she see?

From today's viewpoint, it might appear that all worship in the early church was the same. A Jerusalem worshiper, however, would have been aware of striking differences. Generally, one region's worship differed from another's in several ways: the daily and yearly calendars, the system of Scripture readings, the interpretation of sacraments, the supplemental rites and symbols in administering the sacraments, the architecture, the language spoken, the way in which worship leaders spoke, and how the Bible was used and interpreted, among other things. In the interpretation of sacraments, for example, some churches celebrating baptism would have placed a stronger emphasis upon the death/burial/resurrection motif, whereas others would have emphasized the bestowal of the Holy Spirit, as in Jesus' baptism. Sometimes, too, the supplemental rites and symbols in sacraments could be unique to a place. A Jerusalem worshiper, for instance, would have been quite surprised by northern Italy's addition of a foot-washing during baptism. With respect to how language was used, some regions tended to be concise in their worship speech, whereas others heaped up words and phrases to honor God. Regions also tended to use distinctive phrases and images while praying.

The questions asked by a group of Armenian priests attending the dedication of the newly constructed worship spaces in 335 highlight some of the likely regional differences in the ancient church. Seeking to learn about Jerusalem's practices and appropriate them, the Armenians asked Jerusalem's bishop, Macarius, questions about baptism, the Lord's Supper, and the proper roles of various clergy in worship. Highlighting some of his church's differences, Macarius wrote out an explanation of some practices he wanted the Armenians to adopt. He instructed the Armenians to build baptistries, to give up their practice of using portable basins to baptize. Likewise, Macarius said that deacons ought to have a more limited role in administering sacraments, which would leave the major roles to priests and bishops. Macarius's letter, along with a helpful commentary, can be found in *Macarius of Jerusalem: Letter to the Armenians, A.D. 335,* trans. Abraham Terian (Crestwood, N.Y.: St. Vladimir's Seminary Press; New Rochelle, N.Y.: St. Nersess Armenian Seminary, 2008).

As this example indicates, a Jerusalem worshiper would have been aware of the worldwide diversity in Christian worship, especially because Jerusalem was an increasingly important pilgrimage site. And, over time, a Jerusalem worshiper might have been aware of how worship across Christianity was becoming more uniform as pilgrims brought new practices into the city and then exported practices back to their home churches. A pilgrim from certain parts of the Western church, for example, would have been surprised that Jerusalem commemorated Christ's birth on January 6, not December 25. Likewise, a Jerusalem native might have been intrigued that the Western Christian's church read from John 1 or Luke 2, rather than Matthew 2, to celebrate Christ's birth. Eventually, the West imported the January 6 feast from Jerusalem, resulting in a double Nativity celebration with an emphasis upon the Word Incarnate (John) or the shepherd-oriented birth scene (Luke) on Christmas and the coming of the Magi (Matthew) on **Epiphany**. On a broader basis, as can be seen subsequently in the nun Egeria's travel diary from the 380s (see "A Description of Worship" in Part Two), pilgrims could be mesmerized by how distinctly different aspects of the life of Christ and the biblical story could be commemorated in different venues because of the availability of historical places. Egeria also enthused that the Scripture readings were appropriate for the time and place, suggesting that her native church's worship was not that attentive to correlating readings and occasions. This impression was likely behind the desire in other regions to replicate both the sites (even if in reduced scale or by symbolic representation) one had experienced in Jerusalem's worship and the calendar of services on those sites. For an appraisal of this phenomenon, see Paul F. Bradshaw, "The Influence of Jerusalem on Christian Liturgy," in *Jerusalem: Its Sanctity and Centrality to Judaism, Christianity, and Islam,* ed. Lee I. Levine (New York: Continuum, 1999), pp. 251-59.

With the proliferation of written liturgical texts during this period, one would have been able to see the emergence of families of rites, usually based in geographic regions, like Northern Italy, Spain, or Egypt. (The historian, at least, can see this; it is not clear how much the Jerusalem worshiper would have been aware of this textual phenomenon.) Worship within a region bore a "family resemblance" on the basis of related texts and the practices mentioned above. Relationships between different regional families varied. The main prayer in the Lord's Supper was often the telltale marker of one's belonging to one family of rites or another. For overviews of the different families, see Frank C. Senn, *Christian Liturgy: Catholic and Evangelical* (Minneapolis: Fortress Press, 1997), pp. 115-46, and the entries on liturgical traditions in *The New Dictionary of Sacramental Worship,* ed. Peter Fink (Collegeville, Minn.: Liturgical Press, 1990).

The two closest regional churches, in terms of both geography and likely influence upon Jerusalem, were the churches in Syria and Egypt. Within the categories for these families of rites, scholars often place Jerusalem's worship in the West Syrian family. For analysis of the interactions between the liturgies of these regions, see John F. Baldovin, "A Lenten Sunday Lectionary in Fourth-Century Jerusalem," in *Time and Community: Studies in Liturgical History and Theology,* ed. J. Neil Alexander (Washington: Pastoral Press, 1990), pp. 115-22; G. J. Cuming, "Egyptian Elements in the Jerusalem Liturgy," *Journal of Theological Studies* 25, no. 1 (1974): 117-24; Thomas J. Talley, *The Origins of the Liturgical Year* (New York: Pueblo,

1986); and Bryan D. Spinks, "The Jerusalem Liturgy of the *Catecheses Mystagogicae:* Syrian or Egyptian?" *Studia Liturgica* 18, no. 2 (1989): 391-95. Lawrence J. Johnson's four-volume anthology of historical sources from the patristic period, *Worship in the Early Church* (Collegeville, Minn.: Liturgical Press, 2010), provides liturgically related materials from across early Christianity.

With the fourth century's sharp doctrinal debates over Christ and the Trinity, disputes encompassing the whole Christian world, Jerusalem worshipers would have been aware of bishops and churches considered heretical and with whom fellowship was broken off. Arian churches, who did not say that Christ was fully divine, would have been chief among these. Jerusalem worshipers would have been aware of their church's theological commitment. For one thing, Jerusalem's bishop would have been very attentive to explaining the full divinity of Christ as he taught people prior to their baptisms. Given the doctrinal controversies in the air, the period generally saw a growing attention to the content of liturgical texts, both prayed and sung, to make sure that Christ was honored fully and equally as divine and was not represented as merely subordinate to God the Father. To see how the doctrinal tensions reshaped worship generally, see Jill S. Burnett, "Congregational Song and Doctrinal Formation: The Role of Hymnody in the Arian/Nicene Controversy," *Liturgical Ministry* 10 (Spring 2001): 83-92; Martin F. Connell, "Heresy and Heortology in the Early Church: Arianism and the Emergence of the Triduum," *Worship* 72, no. 2 (March 1998): 117-40; and Joseph A. Jungmann, *The Place of Christ in Liturgical Prayer* (Collegeville, Minn.: Liturgical Press, 1989).

Jerusalem Christians would also have been aware of other worshiping peoples, most notably pagans and Jews. Some scholars have even thought that a majority of the city's population would have been pagan at the time. Pagan worship would have denied the Triune God and the significance of the events in the life of Jesus Christ, which were the bases for Jerusalem's worship. And memories of the pagan emperor Julian, who encouraged Jews to return to Jerusalem and rebuild the Temple in 362, would have been fresh. Regardless of the attempt to rebuild the Temple, most Jewish worship at the time centered on the synagogue, although it is difficult to know much of anything specific about Jewish practices at this time due to lack of contemporary sources. See Michael Avi-Yonah, *The Jews of Palestine* (Oxford: Blackwell, 1976); E. D. Hunt, *Holy Land Pilgrimage in the Later Roman Empire, A.D. 312-460* (New York: Oxford University Press, 1982); Ramsay MacMullen, *Christianity and Paganism in the Fourth to Eighth Centuries* (New Haven: Yale University Press, 1997); Stefan C. Reif, "The Early History of Jewish Worship," in *The Making of Jewish and Christian Worship,* ed. Paul F. Bradshaw and Lawrence A. Hoffman (Notre Dame: University of Notre Dame Press, 1991); and Peter Walker, "Jerusalem and the Holy Land in the Fourth Century," in *The Christian Heritage in the Holy Land,* ed. Anthony O'Mahony (London: Scorpion Cavendish, 1995).

Geographical Landscape

Jerusalem is located on a plateau between the Mediterranean Sea and the Dead Sea. It occupies an important land bridge for traveling between Asia and Africa. In the fourth century, Jerusalem still remained within the eastern portion of the Roman empire.

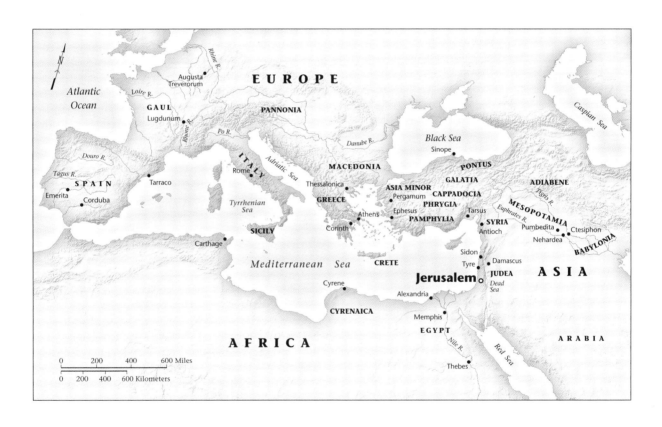

Cautions for Studying Jerusalem's Worship History

Studying the history of ancient practices is difficult because of the limitations of the sources available and the assumptions that individuals bring to them based on personal experiences. Here are a few of the methodological difficulties related specifically to studying worship in this time and place.

- Cyril, Jerusalem's bishop, and Egeria, a pilgrim to that city, are the main sources of information on worship in Jerusalem in the late fourth century. But the descriptions of practices found in Cyril's sermons and Egeria's diary do not always agree. The discrepancy means that exhaustive precision in describing practices is not possible.
- It is not possible to date Cyril's sermons precisely. Some have even questioned his authorship. Since no church's worship is static, it might be that his sermons describe things at a different time than does Egeria's diary.
- Cyril's sermons on the sacraments were not intended to be detailed examinations of these rites. Rather, he was trying to interpret those aspects he thought would be most edifying to the newly baptized. Perhaps there are some important practices he fails to mention.
- Egeria's descriptions are frustratingly short at times, especially when she says that the readings were appropriate for the time and place, without giving further detail, or that the practices were just like those she saw at home. Unfortunately, we do not always know how her home community worshiped.
- Can we be sure that Egeria fully understood everything that was being said or done? If she knew only Latin, she would have had to rely upon finding someone to translate the Greek or Syriac in which the liturgy was conducted. That translation would also have had to have been accurate.
- A person's eye is usually drawn to the novel or unusual. Thus, we can wonder if Egeria tended to describe those things that were new to her and overlooked some important details of the liturgy. Whatever the case may be, Egeria was selective in what she reported.
- Despite its limitations, Egeria's diary is one of the most finely detailed descriptions of worship in a single place for the period. With no comparable document for another church, it is hard to compare and contrast Jerusalem's worship in detail against another locale for the period.

- Available texts of the lectionary or liturgy of St. James are later than the fourth century. There would have been changes and additions after the time of Cyril and Egeria. Thus, these later texts do not always agree with the contemporaneous descriptions found in Cyril or Egeria; what the later texts report should be read back into the fourth century with the greatest caution.

- Because Jerusalem was a major pilgrimage site, Jerusalem's worship was unique in some respects and likely a hybrid of practices brought from around the Christian world. Without the biblical sites and the cross-fertilization brought by pilgrimage, other regions might have experienced different worship in the time period.

Significant Themes and Practices to Observe

As you study the following materials, be on the lookout for these significant themes and practices, which are categorized by some of the primary elements in worship.

Piety

- Worship included reading long passages of Scripture, often chosen to be appropriate for the time and place of worship; people would listen attentively and respond openly.
- Scripture readings were used to remember a Christ-centered story of salvation, which provided the basic content of worship and fueled the people's adoration and devotion.
- Baptism and the Lord's Supper were seen as especially important ways of encountering this biblical story of salvation.

Time

- There were regular rounds of daily, weekly, and yearly worship services.
- The main yearly rhythms focused on Christ's death and resurrection (the **Pascha**/Easter), Christ's birth and his appearing to the nations (Epiphany), and the commemoration of the dedication of the emperor's newly built worship spaces in the city (**Encaenia** in mid-September).
- These yearly celebrations were preceded by periods of ascetic preparation and all-night worship vigils. Yearly celebrations also started seasons of great rejoicing, with the first week being especially important.

Place

- The city of Jerusalem and the surrounding area, near and far, had become filled with buildings which sparked worship focused on events in the biblical story, especially from the life of Christ.
- Even though there was no fixed seating in any of the gathering places, except for certain clergy, there would have been separation of different categories of worshipers (clergy and laity; women and men; monastic and non-monastic).
- Much of Jerusalem's worship was on the move, transitioning in procession from space to space, especially during the yearly celebration of Christ's last week, death, and resurrection.

Prayer

- Prayer life for Christians was very communal rather than private or family-oriented.
- There were regular daily and weekly services for prayer without sermon or sacrament.
- Especially important for the rank-and-file church member were the morning and evening prayer services.

Preaching

- During a single gathering several sermons could be preached back to back, with the bishop presenting the concluding one.
- The Gospel of Jesus Christ provided the basic interpretive lens for preaching all of Scripture.

Music

- Music was perceived not as a separate liturgical action but rather as a way of doing basic acts of worship.
- A choir or soloist assisted congregational singing, which was done without instruments.
- Since it would have been impossible to mass-produce song sheets, the congregation often had a simple, memorable line to sing in response to longer verses sung by practiced voices.
- Psalms were prominent as musical texts.

People

- The worshiping congregations were made up of several different kinds of people: permanent residents of the town, monastics (monks and nuns) who resided there, and pilgrims from across the Christian world.
- Attendance levels seem to have varied by group for different services.
- The preaching and Scripture reading were conducted in Greek and translated into Syriac. Those who understood neither language had to rely upon someone to translate privately for them.
- The bishop was the most important worship leader because of his responsibility for the Word and the Lord's Supper.

PART TWO

Exploring the Worshiping Community

Describing the Community's Worship: Egeria and the Church in Jerusalem, 380s

What follows is a description of worship as it occurred in Jerusalem in the late fourth century. The main source for knowing about this worship is a travel diary kept by a nun named Egeria, who made a pilgrimage. Of particular importance is how the worship in Jerusalem was built upon remembering the places and events in the life of Christ.

She wanted to walk where Jesus walked. Who wouldn't? Even more, she wanted to fulfill Scripture through her worship. Along with numerous other pilgrims to the Holy Land, she probably saw her worship at sites connected to Jesus Christ's life as fulfilling Psalm 132:7: "Let us worship at the place where his feet have stood" (translated from Latin).

She was a nun from the western part of Europe, perhaps from Spain or France. Her name was Egeria. Fulfilling her desire to see the places associated with the stories in the Bible, she took a three-year-long pilgrimage to the Holy Land in the early 380s. At every site Egeria documented her experiences for the sake of her monastic sisters at home. She traveled widely, from Egypt in the West to Abraham's land of origin in the East. But what interested her most were Jerusalem and the surrounding areas, especially where Jesus' life had begun and reached its climax.

Egeria was not alone in her quest. Pilgrimage to the biblical lands had blossomed in the fourth century after the legalization of Christianity. People traveled from across Christendom to see the places associated with scenes from the Old and New Testaments. Many of these locales had newly built worship spaces. Many were part of an expansive program of construction by Constantine, the first Christian emperor, to honor important historical sites. Tombs were also popular sites to visit. Egeria was a typical pilgrim whenever she visited the burial places of biblical figures and Christian martyrs. Another attraction was the number of monastic persons, some famous, who made their home in the region. Many had cells near historical locations and tombs.

Egeria came not primarily to sightsee, but to worship the Lord. Her travel diary records her recurring practice at historic locations. As she traveled across the land, Egeria remembered and worshiped God through biblical stories, prayers, and Psalms appropriate to each place. These on-site worship services included an offering of the Lord's Supper, too, whenever a clergyperson was available. (Egeria's standard way of speaking about Communion was to emphasize not only its receiving but also its offering—*oblatio* in her native Latin.)

The single surviving manuscript of the diary from the eleventh century does not identify its author because only the middle section has survived. But scholars have identified the author as a woman named Egeria mentioned by a seventh-century monk, Valerius. The different manuscripts of Valerius's writings sometimes give variant names for the woman, like Echeria or Aetheria. The eleventh-century manuscript of Egeria's diary was rediscovered in the late nineteenth century.

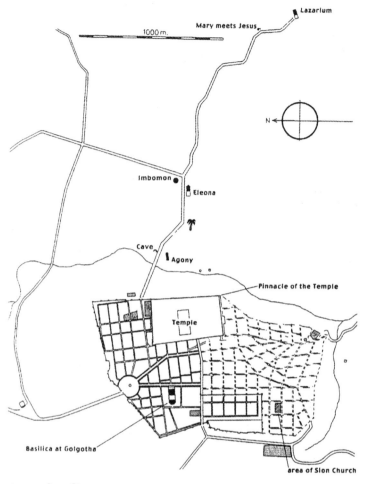

An overview of Jerusalem in the fourth century

Source: John Wilkinson, *Egeria's Travels,* published by Aris & Phillips, 1999

Patristic refers to the first several centuries of church history.

Her excitement, for example, leaps off the page in her description of visiting the top of Mount Sinai, where Moses had received the Law. There—"on the very spot!" she writes—the whole account from Genesis was read, followed by the offering and receiving of the Eucharist.

The high points of Egeria's pilgrimage, however, were her visits to the places associated with Jesus Christ, especially around Jerusalem. The real goal of her pilgrimage was to worship where his feet had stood. Anxious that her sisters might know what liturgy was like in the Holy City, Egeria described it in some detail, providing us with perhaps the most complete firsthand account of a church at worship from the early centuries. Without her report, the modern reader has only bits and pieces from earlier centuries and other churches to suggest how the first Christian congregations adored God. However, Egeria's diary, along with contemporaneous documents and material from slightly later, provides a reasonably thorough picture of a **patristic** church and its liturgy. The irony should not be missed. Just as women provided the first witness to the resurrection of Christ from the grave, a woman provides the best witness to the worship that took place at that grave nearly four hundred years later.

Another irony connected to Jerusalem's worship should not be overlooked. This is the cultural and political distance over which Christianity had traveled since the death of Jesus. Since he had been executed with the complicity of imperial authority, it was paradoxical that imperial authority had constructed the worship spaces that sought to honor the sites of his death, resurrection, and life. But the emperor Constantine's building program in the Holy Land made that happen. He erected places of worship over many of the sites associated with Christ. The crown jewel was the complex raised next to the place of Christ's crucifixion and over the site of his resurrection, the most symbolically important building in church history. Christian worship had come back to where it had started, but this time with visible grandeur.

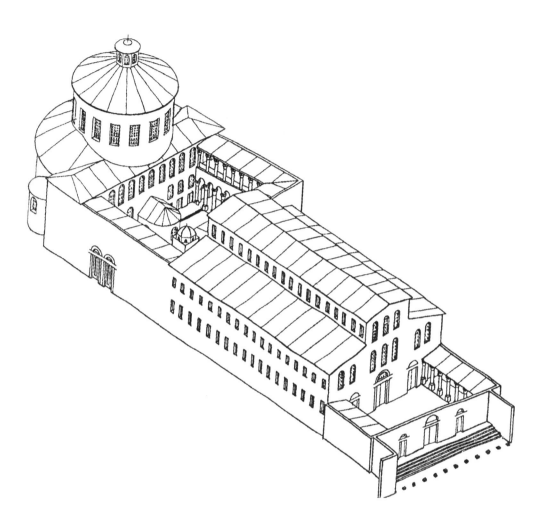

View of the main church complex

Source: John Wilkinson, *Egeria's Travels,* published by Aris & Phillips, 1999

Jerusalem's Christian worship was a watershed in the fourth century.[1] In some respects, it continued practices that reached back to Christianity's pre-legalization days. (Legalization occurred early in the fourth century.) But what happened in Jerusalem also was novel in some ways. Worship's public scale and its linkage with the details of Jesus' life helped establish practices that still exist today. Pilgrims like Egeria helped spread Jerusalem's practices, allowing them to have widespread distribution. Marveling at what they had seen there, the pilgrims helped implement change when they arrived home. They had worshiped where Jesus

1. For a glimpse into what Jerusalem's worship was like in 335 as the Holy Sepulchre complex was dedicated, see *Macarius of Jerusalem: Letter to the Armenians, A.D. 335,* trans. Abraham Terian (Crestwood: St. Vladimir's Seminary Press; New Rochelle, N.Y.: St. Nersess Armenian Seminary, 2008).

walked, lived, and died, and this experience had a profound impact on them. They were eager to re-experience it as best they could in their own churches.

Perhaps what a modern observer would find most striking about the church of Jerusalem was that it moved while it worshiped. Literally. There seems to have been little sense of distinct congregations attached to their own buildings. The whole church in Jerusalem formed one worshiping people. This people ranged across the whole city and its environs, sometimes celebrating in one building and sometimes in another. In this way, Jerusalem's worship was a "colonization of public space" so that worship "provided the public face of Christianity"[2] for most people in the late empire. (The same was true in other cities, too, although perhaps not quite on Jerusalem's grand scale. Scholars call this approach "**stational liturgy**."[3]) While Egeria reported that some services were attended more regularly by one smaller group or another (especially monks and nuns), there was no sense of Jerusalem's Christians feeling as if they belonged to a distinct congregation and building. No Christian there would have said, "Yes, I belong to and worship at the Mount of Olives Church." Indeed, Egeria noted that a Jerusalem worship assembly was an eclectic mix of people, not all of them understanding the same language. The services were conducted in Greek, but a **presbyter**, a church leader a step "below" the bishop, translated into Syriac. Someone in the congregation would translate for those who knew only Latin. Hospitality was important to form a unified worshiping assembly.

Jerusalem Christians had many places to move as they worshiped. The most important set of buildings was the **Holy Sepulcher** complex built on and around the sites of Christ's crucifixion and resurrection. It was principally Constantine who built this complex, although it had further additions by the time Egeria visited it. (A dome over the cave where Christ was buried was perhaps the most important.) In this complex the largest space was the **Martyrium**, a large, rectangular building standard in design for Christian worship spaces at the time and known as a **basilica**. It sat just to the northeast of the rock where Christ had been crucified. The Martyrium (the name comes from a Greek word for witness) was an act of Christian one-upmanship, having been built on the site of a former temple to Aphrodite. To the west of the Martyrium was the **Anastasis** (the Greek word means "resurrection"), the building around the cave where Jesus had been buried. The Anastasis was a round building, with screens and railings that separated spaces for clergy and laypeople. When Egeria saw it, it had been covered with a dome. (The structure around the tomb-chamber, which had been freed on all sides from the rock of its original hillside setting, is called the **edicule**.) A

2. Martin D. Stringer, *A Sociological History of Christian Worship* (Cambridge: Cambridge University Press, 2005), p. 61.

3. The standard work exploring Jerusalem's stational liturgy is John F. Baldovin's *The Urban Character of Christian Worship: The Origins, Development, and Meaning of Stational Liturgy,* Orientalia Christiana Analecta 228 (Rome: Pont. Institutum Studiorum Orientalium, 1987). For a shorter study, see Baldovin's *Liturgy in Ancient Jerusalem,* Alcuin/GROW Liturgical Study 9 (Grove Liturgical Study 57) (Cambridge: Grove Books Limited, 1989). Baldovin provides a narrative description of what a Sunday in Jerusalem would have been like in "Sunday Liturgy in Jerusalem: A Pilgrim's View," in *Worship — City, Church, and Renewal* (Washington: The Pastoral Press, 1991).

courtyard separated the Anastasis from the Martyrium and Golgotha, where Christ had been crucified. In Egeria's time, the rock where the cross had stood was still visible. She also spoke of a forecourt "At the Cross" and a chapel "Behind the Cross." Finally, this complex contained a separate space for baptism, as was common across Christianity. Worship could occur at any of the spaces in the complex or move among them during the same assembly for worship.

Jerusalem Christians had several other places to worship. Within the city itself, there was Sion. This space, located south of the Holy Sepulcher complex, was likely the older site for Christians to worship in the city, predating Constantine's construction program, although a larger, basilica-shaped space had replaced whatever liturgical building had stood there previously. Christians considered it the location for Jesus' resurrection appearances and the outpouring of the Holy Spirit on the first Pentecost. The column on which Jesus had been scourged was there, too. Later Christians also said that the Last Supper took place at the same site.

Immediately to the east of Jerusalem proper was the Mount of Olives, which contained several places for worship. Fourth-century Christians associated these sites with various episodes from Christ's life. The **Eleona** was another basilica-shaped space over the cave where they thought Christ had given some of his last teachings. The Imbomon

An icon of the Bishop Cyril

Source: This icon was painted in egg tempera medium by John Lickwar in 2008. It is part of the Iconostasis at St. Cyril of Jerusalem Orthodox Christian Church in The Woodlands, Texas.

was the site of Christ's ascension to heaven. When Egeria visited, it apparently did not have an enclosed structure over it. Toward the foot of the mount, on the Jerusalem side, was another church built at the site of Christ's prayerful struggles in the Garden of Gethsemane.

Egeria occasionally traveled with other Jerusalem worshipers to churches slightly more remote from the city. One was the **Lazarium**, a worship space built adjacent to the tomb of Lazarus in Bethany. The other was the basilica over the cave in which Jesus Christ had been born in Bethlehem.

Jerusalem's worshipers sometimes participated in large-scale events that involved much place-to-place movement. On certain major holy days, the movement seemed to encompass the whole city. For instance, from the Thursday afternoon before Easter and throughout the next day, Jerusalem's worship transitioned (in order) from the Martyrium, to the chapel behind the cross, to the Anastasis, to the Eleona, to the Imbomon, to the church in Gethsemane, to the **atrium** (the central court or open area at the entrance to the basilica) at the cross, to the column of the scourging at Sion, then back to the chapel behind the Cross, to the atrium at the cross, to the Martyrium, and, finally, to the Anastasis for a service commemorating the burial of Christ.

Another occasion for such large-scale worship came in the weeks after the major celebrations of the year: Easter, Epiphany, and Encaenia. During the first eight days (e.g., Easter Sunday to the following Sunday) of these feasts (known as an **Octave**), worshipers gathered at one of the churches, specially designated, in or around the city. There was a fixed rotation from year to year.

Worshipers moved on a smaller scale, too. Movement through the Holy Sepulcher complex was especially frequent. The main Eucharistic service on Sunday mornings, for example, began in the Martyrium with a complete service of Scripture readings, sermons, prayers, and the Lord's Table, and then moved to the Anastasis immediately afterward for additional prayers and blessings. The buildings were designed for such movement, with multiple doors and neither pews nor seats for the people, who stood as was customary.

When it moved in worship, the church of Jerusalem moved with its bishop. The bishop was the main worship leader because he bore the primary responsibility for the ministries of the Word of God and the sacraments in Jerusalem's worship. These two ministries were the basic building blocks of classic Christian worship. Indeed, "Word and sacrament," in that order, describe the basic order of the central service of worship, both in Jerusalem and in other places of that time period.

In Jerusalem, this order meant that the first part of the service consisted of several Scripture readings from the Old and New Testaments, culminating in a reading from one of the Gospels. Sung Psalms and prayers provided the connection between the readings. After the readings, any presbyter who wanted to had a chance to preach. The bishop's sermon climaxed this part of the service. Note that the bishop would not have done everything, but would have led in worship much like the captain leads on the bridge of a ship, as indicated in a contemporaneous document from Antioch, Syria.

After the ministry of the Word, the service began to direct its attention toward the Lord's Table. Non-baptized worshipers would first be dismissed, which left an assembly of the baptized faithful. These Christians then participated in the service's main intercessory prayers and actions, such as the exchange of peace. The bishop's main responsibility in this second part of the service was to give the main thanksgiving and offering at the table. As with the ministries of Scripture, the bishop did not have to do everything during communion, but he (or a presbyter if the bishop was not there) had the responsibility for this prayer.

In some respects, the bishop's responsibilities for preaching and for praying during sacramental administration were intimately related. Both were recitations of God's saving work through Jesus Christ in the power of the Holy Spirit. The content was essentially the same:

remembrance of God's activity on our behalf. The primary difference was that the sermons were directed toward the people and the prayer was directed as praise toward God.

Indeed, illuminating the close connection of Word and sacrament was seen as one of the bishop's most important liturgical ministries. By explaining what a worshiper experiences in baptism and the Lord's Supper in terms of biblical salvation history, the bishop brought Scripture into close contact with the sacraments. Egeria reported how the bishop, a wise old man named Cyril, taught those who were in final preparation for an Easter baptism for several weeks prior to Easter. (This is the origin for the period we know as **Lent**.)

According to Egeria, Cyril went through the entire story of the Bible, starting with Genesis, and then followed up with a thorough teaching on the Creed as a summary of scriptural faith so that the newly baptized would be able to follow the Scriptures whenever they were read in worship. Thus, one of the bishop's most important liturgical ministries was to immerse baptismal neophytes in the scriptural story so that they could participate well in worship. In like manner, Cyril spent the week after Easter preaching on the meaning of the sacraments that these new Christians had just received. His standard method, not surprisingly, was to use biblical stories to describe the salvation realities they had experienced in baptism and the Lord's Supper. According to the bishop, these baptismal candidates had experienced at the font and the table a story that reached from the primitive glory of Eden through the death and resurrection of Christ. This story Cyril preached while standing where the angels had once stood, at the mouth of Jesus' tomb.

Jerusalem worshipers moved in worship to remember. If Word and sacrament were the fundamental building blocks of worship, then remembrance was the indispensable building block of worship's content. Noticing worship's commemorative content, Egeria enthused that the things said and sung were relevant and appropriate: "And what I admire and value most is that all the hymns and **antiphons** and readings they have, and all the prayers the bishop says, are always relevant to the day which is being observed and to the place in which they are used. They never fail to be appropriate."[4]

Note that Egeria did not determine relevance and appropriateness with reference to the people (Did it meet their felt needs? Did it help them?). Instead, she defined relevance and appropriateness with reference to the sites that witnessed to God's activity in history. Jerusalem's acts of worship were intended to evoke memory in God's people.

Such commemorative worship had not originated in fourth-century Jerusalem. Building prayers of praise and thanksgiving upon rehearsing God's activity, for example, was a long-standing Christian tradition, reaching back to the apostles (see Ephesians 1:3ff. and 1 Peter 1:3ff.) and to Jesus himself (see Matthew 11:25-26 or Luke 10:21). Of course, by praying com-

It is likely that the Jerusalem church baptized on four occasions during the year (Epiphany, Easter, Pentecost, and Encaenia), at least as attested by material from earlier in the fourth century. It is not clear what the pre-baptismal preparation would have been like in the periods prior to Epiphany, Pentecost, and Encaenia.

Antiphons refer to the sung response (refrain) within a musical text.

4. John Wilkinson, *Egeria's Travels* (London: SPCK, 1971; rev. ed., Warminster: Aris & Phillips Ltd., 1999; 3rd ed.), p. 168.

Some ancient liturgical texts became classics and are still used by worshipers today. Below are two examples from the patristic church. The first is a hymn that became standard at evening prayer. Called *Phos Hilaron* (i.e., "Joyful Light"), it was commonly used across the ancient church. The version given below is a recent rendition by the contemporary songwriter Chris Tomlin. The second is a well-known hymn entitled "Let All Mortal Flesh Keep Silence," inspired by the Liturgy of St. James. It is likely that Egeria and Cyril heard versions of both ancient texts in Jerusalem.

Joyous Light*
(Hail Gladdening Light, Revised)

Hail Gladdening Light, sun so bright,
Jesus Christ, end of night, alleluia!
Hail Gladdening Light, Eternal Bright.
In evening time, 'round us shine, alleluia, alleluia!

Hail Gladdening Light, such joyous Light.
O Brilliant Star, forever shine, alleluia, alleluia!

Chorus: We hymn the Father, we hymn the Son.
We hymn the Spirit, wholly Divine.
No one more worthy of songs to be sung.
To the Giver of Life, all glory is Thine.

Let All Mortal Flesh Keep Silence

Let all mortal flesh keep silence, and with fear and trembling stand;
Ponder nothing earthly minded, for with blessing in His hand,
Christ our God to earth descendeth, our full homage to demand.

King of kings, yet born of Mary, as of old on earth He stood,
Lord of lords, in human vesture, in the body and the blood,
He will give to all the faithful His own self for heavenly food.

Rank on rank the host of heaven spreads its vanguard on the way,
As the Light of Light descendeth, from the realms of endless day,
That the powers of hell may vanquish as the darkness clears away.

At His feet the six-winged seraph; Cherubim, with sleepless eye,
Veil their faces to the presence, as with ceaseless voice they cry,
Alleluia, Alleluia, Alleluia, Lord Most High!

memoratively, the apostles and Jesus were honoring their own Jewish roots extending back to the Old Testament.

Even if Jerusalem did not create commemorative worship, it did carry it to a new degree of thoroughness, as compared to other regions at the time. Egeria was not simply reporting what she had seen but was truly marveling at how much the Scriptures fit the time and place, as if this level of connection experienced in Jerusalem was something she had not encountered previously. Surely part of this novelty was the association of liturgical commemoration with specific historic places and the churches that had been built there. This was where Jerusalem had an "advantage" over the rest of the Christian world. The abundance of sites connected to different episodes of salvation history meant that worship commemorations had the potential for becoming more distinct and isolated, less a part of an integrated whole that held together the entire sweep of that history as one story. Egeria's diary documented a trajectory for worship heading in that direction, although later centuries would see this trajectory elevated to a significantly greater level.

In Jerusalem, commemoration was connected not only to space but also to time. As Egeria commented repeatedly, the appropriateness of the acts of worship in Jerusalem was connected to both the place and the date. She reported on discernible rhythms in time for the day, the week, and the year, with perhaps the stronger commemorative elements tied to the week and to the year. Worship in Jerusalem was a little like a dance conducted over a large space. Jerusalem worshipers moved in time with the bishop.

For example, on Sundays, the bishop, Cyril, arrived to lead a service in the Anastasis before dawn. As he entered, all the doors were opened, and worshipers streamed into the space, which was bright with blazing lamps. (Before the bishop's arrival, people had already gathered in the courtyard beside the Anastasis and had begun to worship.) Three psalms were sung in such a way that all could participate (the use of a recurring refrain or antiphon allowed that in a time when there were no church bulletins or projection equipment), with prayers interspersed between them. A broad intercessory prayer followed. Following that, censers were taken into the cave so that the their sweet smell drifted out to fill the whole space. The bishop then stepped forward to stand inside the screen at the entrance of the cave. There he read a long passage from the Gospel that seemed to cover the time from Christ's passion to his resurrection. Afterward, the people, singing, accompanied the bishop to the site of the cross. A final psalm, prayer, and blessing concluded this short vigil. Some stayed, continuing psalms and prayers, but most returned home for a short rest before the main service of Word and sacrament that began at daybreak in the Martyrium. This was the start of the weekly "dance" of remembrance in time and space in Jerusalem's worship.

Moving to yearly rhythms was perhaps an even more prominent feature in Jerusalem's worship. The number of special annual celebrations, most tied to the life of Christ, had increased considerably in the fourth century. At the beginning of the century there were few feast days. But by the time Egeria visited Jerusalem in the 380s, a liturgical calendar had emerged. Jerusalem began with Epiphany, a mid-winter remembrance of the birth of Christ as the manifestation of God. Forty days after the birth of Christ, Jerusalem commemorated the presentation of Jesus in the Temple. Next came an extended period of fasting and preparation to renew the church and prepare candidates for an Easter baptism. Egeria said the local name was *Heortae;* other Christians called it Lent. The week before Easter remembered the last events in Jesus' life, beginning with the raising of Lazarus and the palm entrance into Jerusalem. After the almost non-stop worship of Thursday and Friday of that week, worshipers got a brief break on Saturday before an all-night vigil climaxing with worship on Resurrection morning. Fifty days later, on Pentecost, another round of services rejoiced in the outpouring of the Holy Spirit and Christ's ascension to heaven.

The uniqueness of these yearly rhythms should not be overlooked. The development of the calendar was one of the most significant liturgical developments in the fourth century. At the beginning of the century, the typical Christian worshiper would have been most attuned to daily and weekly rhythms, with the only annual celebration likely being an integrated remembrance of Christ's passing over from death to life. By the end of the century, however, the church had developed virtually the same liturgical calendar that churches use now. Jerusalem was instrumental in establishing these rhythms—and some of their particular practices—across Christianity.

Jerusalem worshipers were moved emotionally by their worship, mirrored by how they moved outwardly in its rhythms of time and space. Egeria depicted how deeply people's affections could be touched in worship, thereby dispelling any notion we might have that the early church's worship was staid and stuffy because it involved a great deal of ceremony. Egeria drew a picture of worship in which people wept, shouted, called back to the preacher, and applauded with delight.

What moved Jerusalem's worshipers so? It was the story of God's deeds for humanity. Every instance of strong emotional response from the congregation portrayed by Egeria came either when Scripture was read or when a sermon was delivered. It happened every Sunday morning in the Anastasis when the bishop read the Scripture about Christ's resurrection. It happened during the Lenten teaching as the bishop recounted the story of salvation in Scripture and in the creed to prepare candidates for baptism. It happened on the Friday before Easter as the people, gathered in the early darkness in Gethsemane, heard the Gospel account of Christ's arrest. It happened later that day in the courtyard before the cross, when the Old Testament readings predicted the Savior's suffering and the New Testament readings showed their fulfillment in his death. And it happened during the week after Easter as the bishop stood in the entry of Christ's tomb and proclaimed that the newly baptized had been incorporated into God's mighty acts of salvation.

Pointing to things like the dramatic ceremonies, Cyril's creative use of space, and the secrecy that surrounded the sacraments, scholars have noted that Jerusalem's worship was awe-inspiring. Egeria even remarked on the splendor of the buildings and the opulence of their decorations. But it was only in the ministries of the Word read and proclaimed that Egeria described the worshiping congregation as having an overt emotional response. They loved the Story and were moved by it.

Documenting the Community's Worship

PEOPLE AND ARTIFACTS

A Posture of Prayer in the Early Church
Standing with hands and eyes upraised was a common posture for prayer in the early church. Although this portrayal dates from the late third century and from a different place than Jerusalem, such portrayals can help one imagine what it would have been like for Jerusalem's buildings to have been filled with worshipers. Envision, for example, hundreds with hands upraised, gathered around the tomb of Christ.

Source: Lunette with Orante. From early Christian fresco, second half of the third century. Catacomb of Priscilla, Rome, Italy. Photo credit: Scala/Art Resource, NY

A Fresco of Constantine's Mother

Helen or Helena, considered a saint in both Eastern and Western churches, was the wife of
Emperor Constantius, to whom she bore a son, Constantine. She was later divorced by Constantius for political reasons, but Constantine raised her to a position of great honor when
he became emperor in 306. About 325, she traveled to the Holy Land, founded important
churches and, according to later legend, discovered the relic of the cross of Christ.

Source: Saint Helen, mother of Emperor Constantine the Great. Fresco in Elmali Kilise in Goreme.
Byzantine, 11 C.E. Cappadocia, Turkey. Photo credit: Gilles Mermet/Art Resource, NY

A Bust of Constantine

Constantine, also known as Constantine I or Constantine the Great, was the son of Helena and the Emperor Constantius Chlorus. He was born sometime in the 270s or 280s. In 306, upon the death of Constantius, he was proclaimed emperor. In 312 he became senior ruler of the Roman Empire after defeating Maxentius, his rival, at the Milvian Bridge. This victory marked Constantine's adoption of Christianity, and for the remainder of his reign he supported and promoted it.

Source: Emperor Constantine the Great (reigning from 306-337 C.E.). Marble head, fragment of a colossal statue (overall height 12 m) from the Basilica of Constantine in Rome, now in the courtyard of the Palazzo dei Conservatori, Rome. Musei Capitolini, Rome, Italy. Photo credit: Erich Lessing/Art Resource, NY

The Baptism of Constantine

This twelfth-century portrayal shows Constantine being baptized by Pope Sylvester, a legend that arose in the fifth century. In actuality, Constantine was probably baptized just before his death in 337, a common occurrence at the time. His acceptance of Christianity early in the fourth century, however, made possible a stunning change in the relationship between church and state, which made the fourth century one of dramatic changes in worship.

Source: *The Baptism of Constantine the Great by Pope Silvester I.* Roundel from the left wing of the Stavelot Triptych. Mosan, c. 1156-1158. The Pierpont Morgan Library, New York, NY. Photo credit: The Pierpont Morgan Library/Art Resource, NY

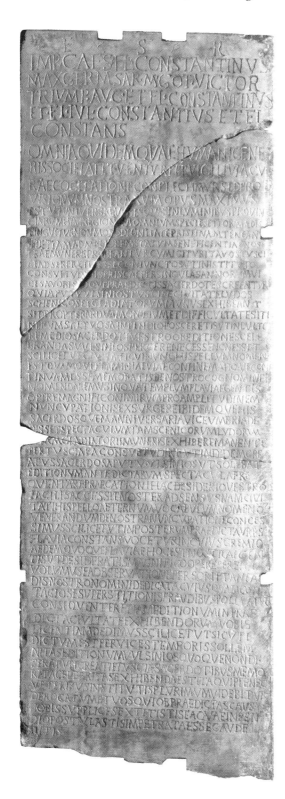

A Fourth-Century Imperial Edict of Constantine Inscribed in Stone

Although not directly related to the issues in this volume, this tablet exemplifies the power Constantine would have exercised as emperor. With Constantine, the weight of the Roman Empire shifted from being arrayed against the church (Constantine was old enough to be aware of the emperor Diocletian's savage persecution of Christians in 303) to being aligned with it.

Source: Edicto of Constantine the Great granting favors. Roman, 4th C.E. Location: Palazzo Comunale, Spello, Italy, Photo credit: Scala/Art Resource, NY

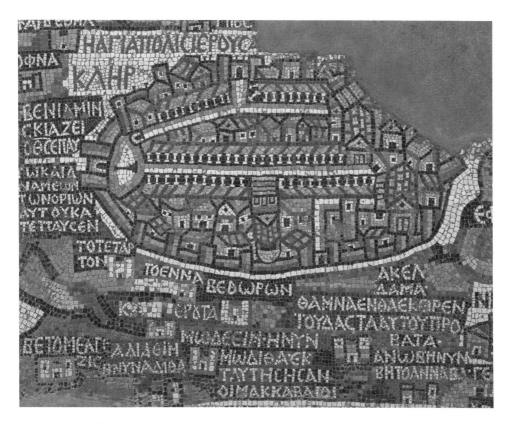

An Early Map of Jerusalem

This sixth-century mosaic, found in a church in Madaba, Jordan, is perhaps the earliest visual portrayal of Jerusalem after the building program of the fourth century. The buildings surrounding the Holy Sepulcher are clearly visible in the center of this map; the Anastasis dome is in the middle and points to the bottom of the image. The white line moving left to right in the center of the mosaic is the Cardo Maximum, one of the main roads through Jerusalem at the time. The Holy Sepulcher complex lay on that road.

The Various Buildings of the Holy Sepulcher Complex with Original Landscape
This conjectural drawing shows the entire Holy Sepulcher complex from the northwest. The drawing reflects the status of the complex in the second half of the fourth century and shows its relationship to the original terrain. This bird's-eye view shows the major buildings of the complex and their relative position to one another. From left to right (east to west), one can see depicted here the main street which fronted the complex, the outer atrium for gathering, the basilica known as the Martyrium, Golgotha (Calvary), the inner atrium before the Anastasis, the Anastasis (the building over Christ's tomb), and then the baptistry which adjoined the inner atrium. Services could be held at one of these locations or move between multiple locations, whether here or spread across the city.

1 Martyrium basilica

2 Golgotha

3 The center of the Rotunda and the dome above, focused on the tomb entrance, the spot where the risen Christ stepped out from death to life, as expressed by Constantine's architects

4 Colonnaded street

5 Outer atrium

6 Inner atrium

7 Cave of the Anastasis

8 Rotunda

9 Hill (cut out)

10 Ground study (probable) A.D. 29-30

11 Possible other tombs within similar rock

12 Baptistry

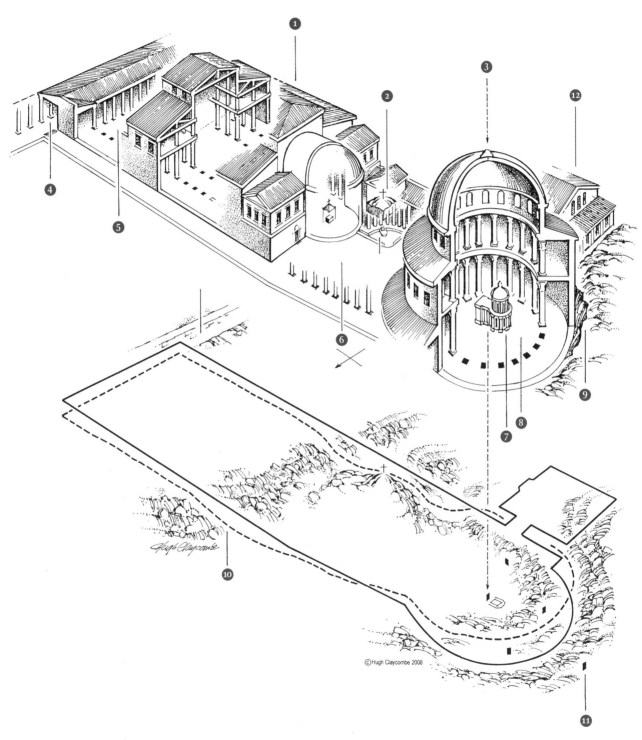

© Hugh Claycombe 2010

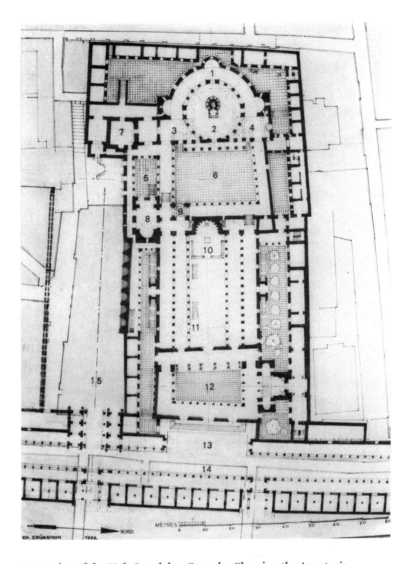

A Drawing of the Holy Sepulcher Complex Showing the Anastasis
This drawing gives a bird's-eye view of the main complex of worship buildings in Jerusalem.
(Precise reconstructions of these spaces are impossible; this is an approximation.) Construction of this complex was the centerpiece of Emperor Constantine's architectural endeavors
in the city. The main thoroughfare (Cardo Maximus) is at the bottom of the drawing. Moving
upward from this main road, one can see, in order, the entrance to and atrium of the basilica,
the basilica itself (called the Martyrium), the cross, the courtyard next to the Anastasis and
the cross, and the Anastasis itself.

Source: Image copyright © The British Academy, 1974. Reproduced by permission from the Schweich Lectures
of the British Academy, 1972.

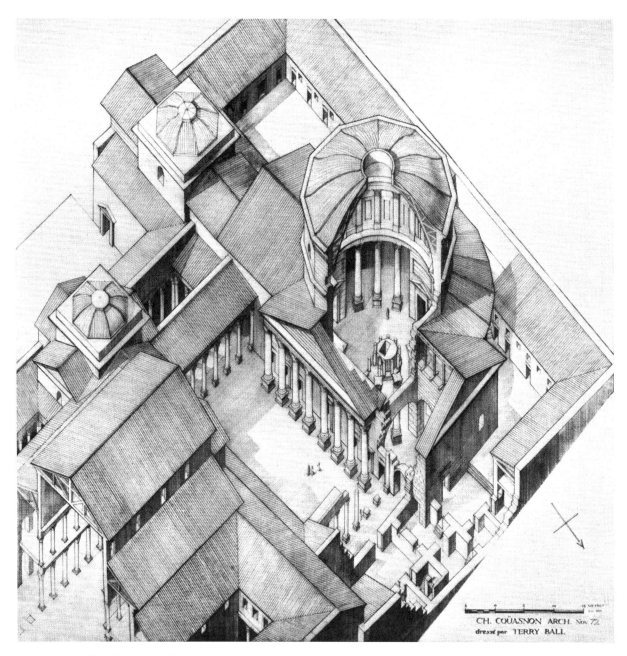

A Reconstruction of the Worship Space over Christ's Tomb

This reconstruction is a cutaway view of what the worship space around Christ's tomb, the Anastasis, might have looked like. The basilica known as the Martyrium is in the lower left-hand corner.

The Rotunda of the Anastasis

This conjectural side view gives a sense of the size of the monument at Christ's tomb as well as the rotunda which covered the tomb. One should imagine the excitement that would swell the congregation as the bishop stepped to the mouth of the tomb every Sunday morning and read the account of Christ's passage from death to life.

1 Entry

2 Tomb space

3 This is the only chunk of bedrock remaining from the original tomb which had been cut into the hillside for Joseph of Arimathea, and is presumed to be the surface upon which Christ's body had been placed.

4 Cave of the Anastasis (after Conant)

5 Rock cut for rotunda

6 Original rock hill unknown

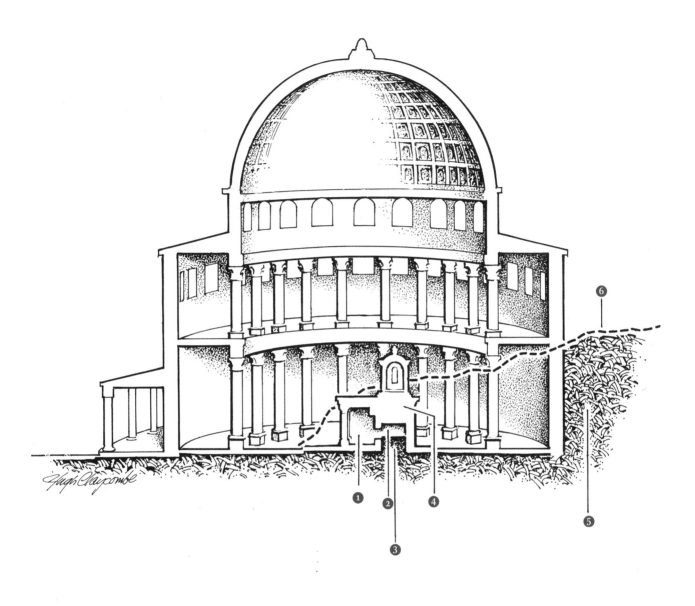

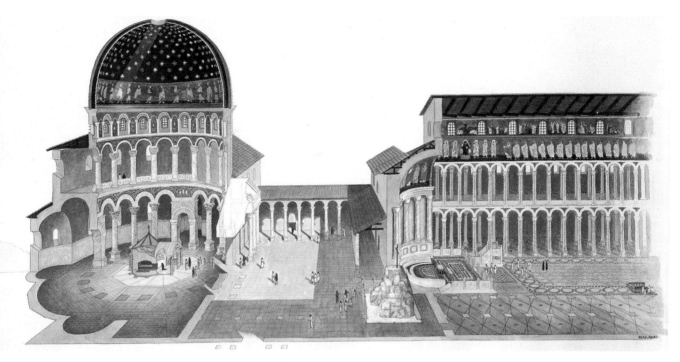

The Holy Sepulcher Complex from the South

This cutaway conjectural drawing shows the complex from the south. The viewpoint places the viewer near the top of the ancient baptistery. On the left is the Anastasis with the tomb of Christ at the center. Calvary is in the right center foreground. The Martyrium is the structure on the right. The artist's reconstruction with human figures shows how the spacious complex was well-suited for gatherings and processions.

Source: The Israel Museum, Jerusalem, by Balage, after the exhibition catalogue "Cradle of Christianity"

Another Reconstruction of the Worship Space over Christ's Tomb

This is another view of what Christ's tomb (the structure around it is called the edicule) in the Anastasis might have looked like. In this artist's reconstruction, one can see the outer porch and the tomb-chamber behind it, freed from its original hillside.

Source: The Israel Museum, Jerusalem, by Balage, after the exhibition catalogue "Cradle of Christianity"

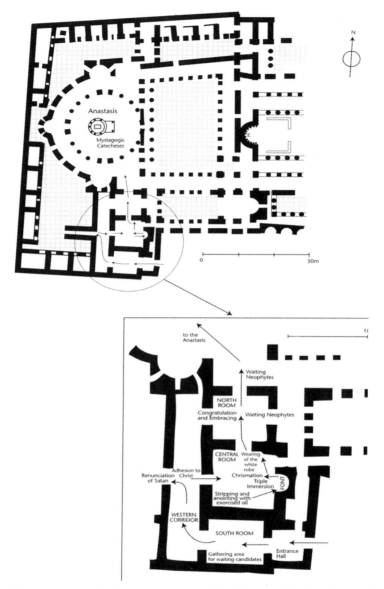

A Close-up View of the Anastasis over Christ's Tomb with the Itinerary for Those Being Baptized
The inset here gives a detailed view of the baptistry attached to the Anastasis and of the places at
which different parts of the baptismal rites were conducted. Several different ceremonies were
conducted with each candidate during baptism. By the end of the ceremonies, the candidate's
whole body had been involved in order to symbolize different aspects of salvation. (See Cyril's
sermons in this volume for specific details.) Notice that the newly baptized would visit the tomb
of Christ in the Anastasis before rejoining the worshiping congregation in the Martyrium.

Source: Image copyright © The British Academy, 1974. Reproduced by permission from the Schweich Lectures
of the British Academy, 1972

A Description of Worship

Egeria's Diary: A Pilgrim's Observations of Jerusalem at Worship

Egeria's diary is one of the fullest firsthand accounts of worship in this period. It begins with her travels in the Middle East. Our excerpts pick up the account directly after Egeria recounts taking a journey from Antioch to Constantinople. She travels along the coast to Isauria, where she visits the martyrium in St. Thecla and one of her friends, a deaconess named Marthana. She concludes this section by planning a further pilgrimage to Ephesus. At this point in the diary, Egeria begins describing the worship she experienced in Jerusalem. This account starts with her description of the round of daily prayer services, especially for monks and nuns. Notice that some of these excerpts involve the presence of the bishop with an entourage of clergy, and some do not. The services with the bishop are probably different with respect to content and the selection of the Psalms. The numbering provided here reflects the paragraph and sentence numbering used in scholarly books.

Although this is one of the best firsthand accounts of worship from the fourth century, Egeria's diary is not without its difficulties as a historical record. For one thing, it doesn't always match information found in other sources like Cyril's sermons. Is this because Egeria didn't always understand what was being said or done? Or, if she had provided more than her at times all-too-brief summary, could we better see how it fits with other historical records? Maybe her eye was drawn to the novel or unique, whereas Cyril wanted to stress what was most pastorally beneficial. Perhaps changes were coming quickly at the time, and thus even a few years' separation between different historical records would create discrepancies. Nonetheless, what we find in Egeria's writings is one of the best on-the-ground accounts of worship from the early church.

24

1 Loving sisters, I am sure it will interest you to know about the daily services they have in the holy places, and I must tell you about them. All the doors of the Anastasis are opened before cock-crow each day, and the "***monazontes* and *parthenae*,**" as they call them here, come in, and also some lay men and women, at least those who are willing to wake at such an early hour. From then until daybreak they join in singing the refrains to the hymns, psalms, and antiphons. There is a prayer between each of the hymns, since there are two or three presbyters and deacons that take each day by turns to be there with the *monazontes* and say the prayers between all the hymns and antiphons.

2 As soon as dawn comes, they start the Morning Hymns, and the bishop with his clergy comes and joins them. He goes straight into the cave. Inside the railed area he first says the Prayer for All (mentioning any names he wishes) and blesses the **catechumens**. Then

Monazontes and *parthenae* refer to monks and nuns.

The cave refers to the tomb of Christ; the screen was at its entrance.

A catechumen is someone preparing to be baptized.

he says another prayer and blesses the faithful. Then he comes outside the railed area, and everyone comes up to kiss his hand. He blesses them one by one, and goes out. By the time the dismissal takes place, it is already day.

3   Again at midday everyone comes into the Anastasis and says psalms and antiphons until a message is sent to the bishop. Again he enters, and, without taking his seat, goes straight inside the railed area in the Anastasis (which is to say into the cave where he went in the early morning), and again, after a prayer, he blesses the faithful and comes outside the railed area, and again they come to kiss his hand.

Lucernare is an evening prayer service, named because of the role of the lights. The name comes from the Latin *lux,* the word for light.

4   At three o'clock they do once more what they did at midday, but at four o'clock they have *Lychnicon,* as they call it, or in our language, **Lucernare.** All the people congregate once more in the Anastasis, and the lamps and candles are all lit, which makes it very bright. The fire is brought not from outside, but from the cave—inside the railed area—where a lamp is always burning night and day. For some time they have the Lucernare psalms and antiphons; then they send for the bishop, who enters and sits in the chief seat. The presbyters also come and sit in their places, and the hymns and antiphons go on.

5   Then, when they have finished singing everything which is appointed, the bishop rises and goes in front of the railed area (i.e., the railed area before the tomb of Christ). One of the deacons makes the normal commemoration of individuals, and each time he mentions a name, a large group of boys responds *Kyrie eleison* (in our language, "Lord, have mercy"). Their voices are very loud.

6   As soon as the deacon has done his part, the bishop says a prayer and prays the Prayer for All. Up to this point the faithful and the catechumens are praying together, but now the deacon calls every catechumen to stand where he is and bow his head. The bishop says the blessing over the catechumens from his place. There is another prayer, after which the deacon calls for all the faithful to bow their heads, and the bishop says the blessing over the faithful from his place. Thus the dismissal takes place at the Anastasis, and they all come up one by one to kiss the bishop's hand.

7   Then, singing hymns, they take the bishop from the Anastasis to the Cross, and everyone goes with him. On arrival he says one prayer and blesses the catechumens, then another and blesses the faithful. Then again the bishop and all the people go behind the Cross, and do there what they did before the Cross. In both places they come to kiss the bishop's hand, as they did in the Anastasis. Great glass lanterns are burning everywhere, and there are many candles in front of the Anastasis, and also before and behind the Cross. By the end of all this, it is dusk. So these are the services held every weekday at the Cross and at the Anastasis.

Each Sunday morning begins at the tomb of Jesus Christ. Remembering his resurrection is the starting point for the Christian sense of time in worship.

8   But on the seventh day, the Lord's Day, there gather in the courtyard before cock-crow all the people, as many as can get in, as if it was Easter. The courtyard is the "basilica" beside the Anastasis, that is to say, out of doors, and lamps have been hung there for them.

Those who are afraid they may not arrive in time for cock-crow come early and sit, waiting there while singing hymns and antiphons. In between, they have prayers. There are always presbyters and deacons there ready for the vigil because so many people collect there, and it is not usual to open the holy places before cock-crow.

9   Soon the first cock crows, and at that the bishop enters and goes into the cave in the Anastasis. The doors are all opened, and all the people come into the Anastasis, which is already ablaze with lamps. When they are inside, a psalm is said by one of the presbyters, with everyone responding, and it is followed by a prayer. Then a psalm is said by one of the deacons and another prayer. Then a third psalm is said by one of the clergy, a third prayer, and the Commemoration of All.

10   After these three psalms and prayers, they take censers into the cave of the Anastasis, so that the whole Anastasis basilica is filled with the smell. Then the bishop, standing inside the railed area, takes the Gospel book and goes to the door, where he himself reads the account of the Lord's resurrection. At the beginning of the reading, the whole assembly groans and laments at all the Lord underwent for us, and the way they weep would move even the hardest heart to tears.

> This long reading of Scripture shows that remembering Christ's death and resurrection is the foundation of weekly worship. The people respond emotionally to this recounting.

11   When the Gospel is finished, the bishop comes out and is taken with singing to the Cross. Everyone goes with him. They have one psalm there and a prayer; then he blesses the people, and that is the dismissal. As the bishop goes out, everyone comes to kiss his hand.

12   Then straightaway the bishop retires to his house, and all the *monazontes* go back into the Anastasis to sing psalms and antiphons until daybreak. There are prayers between all these psalms and antiphons, and presbyters and deacons take their turn every day at the Anastasis to keep vigil with the people. Some lay men and women like to stay on there till daybreak, but others prefer to go home again to bed for some sleep.

> Here's an instance when monastics, compared with common worshipers, continue in a more extended period of worship.

25

1   At daybreak the people assemble in the Great Church built by Constantine on Golgotha behind the Cross. It is the Lord's Day, and they do what is everywhere the custom on the Lord's Day. But you should note that here it is usual for any presbyter who has taken his seat to preach, if he so wishes, and when they have finished there is a sermon from the bishop. The object of having this preaching every Sunday is to make sure that the people will continually be learning about the Bible and the love of God. Because of all the preaching, it is a long time before the dismissal, which takes place not before ten or even eleven o'clock.

2   And when the dismissal has taken place in the church—in the way which is usual everywhere—the *monazontes* lead the bishop with singing to the Anastasis. While they are sing-

ing and the bishop approaches, all the doors of the Anastasis basilica are opened, and the people (not the catechumens, only the faithful) all go in.

3   When they are all inside, the bishop enters, and passes straight inside the railed area of the tomb, the cave itself. They have a thanksgiving to God and the Prayer for All. Then the deacon calls every single person to bow his head, and the bishop blesses them from his place inside the railed area.

4   Then he comes out, and, as he does so, everyone comes to kiss his hand. Thus the dismissal is delayed till almost eleven or twelve o'clock.

Lucernare is held in the same way as on other days. Except on the special days, which we shall be describing below, this order is observed every day of the year.

5   What I found most impressive about all this was that the psalms and antiphons they use are always appropriate, whether at night, in the early morning, at the day prayers, at midday or three o'clock, or at Lucernare. Everything is suitable, appropriate, and relevant to what is being done.

6   Every Sunday in the year except one they assemble in the Great Church which Constantine built on Golgotha behind the Cross. The exception is Pentecost, the Fiftieth Day after Easter, when they assemble on Sion. You will find this mentioned below, but what they do is to go to Sion before nine o'clock after their dismissal in the Great Church … [Unfortunately, part of the diary manuscript is missing at this point.]

… "Blessed is he that cometh in the name of the Lord," and so on. They have to go slowly for the sake of the *monazontes* who are on foot, so they arrive in Jerusalem almost at daybreak, but just before it is light, at the moment when people can first recognize each other.

27

1   Then comes the Easter season, and this is how it is kept. In our part of the world we observe forty days before Easter, but here they keep eight weeks. It makes eight weeks because there is no fasting on the Sundays or the Saturdays (except one of them, which is a fast because it is the Easter vigil—but apart from that the people here never fast on any Saturday in the year). So the eight weeks, less eight Sundays and seven Saturdays—one being a fasting Saturday—make forty-one fast days. The local name for Lent is *Heortae*.

2   Here is what is done on each of these weeks. On Sundays the bishop reads the Gospel of the Lord's resurrection at first cock-crow, as he does on every Sunday throughout the year. Then, till daybreak, they do everything as they would on an ordinary Sunday at the Anastasis and the Cross. In the morning they assemble (as they do every Sunday) in the Great Church called the Martyrium on Golgotha behind the Cross, and do what it is usual to do on a Sunday.

3   After the dismissal in this church they go singing, as they do every Sunday, to the Anasta-

Prayer services without Eucharist or sermon were a standard part of Jerusalem's daily and weekly worship, even when time did allow for the sacrament.

Egeria is familiar with Lent lasting a shorter period of time in her home church. The difference seems to be that Jerusalem did not fast on Saturdays and thus Saturdays did not count as part of Lent. Among scholars, the duration of Lent as described by Egeria is controversial in that it is difficult to reconcile with other accounts of Jerusalem's practice in the late fourth and early fifth centuries.

sis, and it is after eleven o'clock by the time they have finished. Lucernare is at the normal time when it always takes place in the Anastasis and at the Cross and in all the other holy places; for on Sundays there is no service at three o'clock.

4   At first cock-crow on Monday people go to the Anastasis, and till morning they do what is normal during the rest of the year. Then at nine o'clock they go to the Anastasis and do what during the rest of the year would be done at noon, since this service at nine o'clock is added during Lent. The services at noon and three o'clock, and Lucernare, are held as usual in the holy places all the year round.

5   On Tuesday everything is done as on Monday, and on Wednesday they again go on to the Anastasis while it is still night, and follow the usual order till morning, and so at nine o'clock and midday. But at three o'clock they assemble on Sion, because all through the year they regularly assemble on Sion at three o'clock on Wednesdays and Fridays. On those days there is fasting even for catechumens, unless they coincide with a martyrs' day, and this is their reason for assembling on Sion at three o'clock. But even on a martyrs' day they still assemble on Sion at three o'clock if it also happens to be a Wednesday or Friday in Lent.

6   On Wednesdays in Lent, then, they assemble, as during the rest of the year, at three o'clock on Sion, and have all the things usual for the hour, except the Offering. The bishop and the presbyter are at pains to preach, to ensure that the people will continue to learn God's Law. And after the dismissal the people conduct the bishop with singing to the Anastasis, starting out in time to arrive at the Anastasis for Lucernare. They have the hymns and antiphons, and the Lucernare dismissal takes place at the Anastasis and the Cross.

> This narrative highlights the many levels of engagement possible for worshipers.

7   Though during Lent it is later than at other times of the year. Thursday is exactly like Monday and Tuesday, and Friday like Wednesday since they again go to Sion at three o'clock and from there conduct the bishop with singing to the Anastasis. But from the time of their procession from Sion on Friday there is a vigil service in the Anastasis until the early morning. It lasts from the time of Lucernare till the morning of the next day (Saturday), and they make the Offering in the Anastasis so early that the dismissal takes place before sunrise.

> When Egeria speaks of the Offering, she is referring to the celebration of Communion. By using this term, she emphasizes the Lord's Supper as giving to God by following his command to do so in remembrance.

8   Throughout the night they have psalms with refrains or antiphons, or various readings, and this goes on till morning. So in the Saturday service, the Offering, in the Anastasis, is before sunrise, by which I mean at the time when the sun begins to rise, the dismissal has already taken place in the Anastasis. That is how they keep each week of Lent.

9   They have the Saturday service as early as this, before sunrise, so that the people here called hebdomadaries can break their fast as soon as possible. The Lenten fasting rule for these hebdomadaries (people who "keep a week") is that they may eat on a Sunday— when the dismissal is at eleven in the morning. And since their Sunday meal is the last they will have had, and they cannot eat till Saturday morning, they receive Communion

early on Saturday. So the Saturday service at the Anastasis takes place before sunrise for the sake of these people, so that they can break their fast all the sooner. But when I say that the service is early because of them, it is not that I mean that they are the only ones to receive Communion. Anyone who wishes may make his Communion in the Anastasis on Saturdays.

29

Following the timing from the Gospel of John (chapter 12), the worship of Jerusalem's church moves outside the city to Bethany, the home of Lazarus, whom Jesus raised from the dead. The site would be associated not only with that miracle but also with Mary's anointing of Jesus' feet in conjunction with his pending burial.

3   At dawn on Saturday morning the bishop makes the usual Saturday morning Offering. Then, for the dismissal, the archdeacon makes this announcement: "At one o'clock today let us all be ready at the Lazarium." Just at one o'clock everyone arrives at the Lazarium, which is Bethany, about two miles from the city.

4   About half a mile before you get to the Lazarium from Jerusalem there is a church by the road. It is the spot where Lazarus's sister Mary met the Lord. All the monks meet the bishop when he arrives there, and the people go into the church. They have one hymn, an antiphon, and a reading from the Gospel about Lazarus's sister meeting the Lord. Then, after a prayer, everyone is blessed, and they go on with singing to the Lazarium.

5   By the time they arrive there so many people have collected that they fill not only the Lazarium itself, but all the fields around. They have hymns and antiphons which—like all the readings—are suitable to the day and the place. Then at the dismissal a presbyter announces Easter. He mounts a platform and reads the Gospel passage which begins "When Jesus came to Bethany six days before the Passover..." After this reading, with its announcement of Easter, comes the dismissal.

6   They do it on this day because the Gospel describes what took place in Bethany "six days before the Passover," and it is six days from this Saturday to the Thursday night on which the Lord was arrested after the Supper. Thus they all return to the Anastasis and have Lucernare in the usual way.

30

The Great Week is the week preceding Easter, filled with special worship services every day that commemorate the last week of Christ's life.

What Egeria labels as the start of Great Week is now popularly known as Palm Sunday.

1   The next day, Sunday, is the beginning of the Easter week or, as they call it here, "The **Great Week.**" On this Sunday they do everything as usual at the Anastasis and the Cross from cock-crow to daybreak, and then as usual assemble in the Great Church known as the Martyrium because it is on Golgotha behind the Cross, where the Lord was put to death.

2   When the service in the Great Church has taken place in the usual way, before the dismissal, the archdeacon makes this announcement: "During this week, starting tomorrow, let us meet at three in the afternoon at the Martyrium" (that is, in the Great Church). And he makes another announcement: "At one o'clock today let us be ready on the Eleona."

3   After the dismissal in the Great Church, the Martyrium, the bishop is taken with sing- ing to the Anastasis. They do in the Anastasis the things which usually follow the Sunday dismissal in the Martyrium. Then everyone goes home and eats a quick meal, so as to be ready by one o'clock at the Eleona church on the Mount of Olives, the place of the cave where the Lord used to teach.

> The times Egeria refers to are different times during the day for prayer services, called an "office."

31

1   At one o'clock all the people go up to Eleona Church on the Mount of Olives. The bishop takes his seat, and they have hymns and antiphons suitable to the place and the day, and readings too. When three o'clock comes, they go up with hymns and sit down at the Imbomon, the place from which the Lord ascended into heaven. (For when the bishop is present everyone is told to sit down, except for the deacons, who remain standing the whole time.) And there too they have hymns and antiphons suitable to the place and the day, with readings and prayers between them.

> The ability to worship at the sites described in biblical episodes allows the first hints of dramatization in worship. Here is a degree of literal re-enactment of the biblical event. This is different than the kind of sacramental participation that Cyril describes in his sermons.

2   At five o'clock the passage is read from the Gospel about the children who met the Lord with palm branches, saying, "Blessed is he that cometh in the name of the Lord."

At this the bishop and all the people rise from their places, and start off on foot down from the summit of the Mount of Olives. All the people go before him with psalms and antiphons, all the time repeating, "Blessed is he that cometh in the name of the Lord."

3   The babies and the ones too young to walk are carried on their parents' shoulders. Every- one is carrying branches, either palm or olive, and they accompany the bishop in the very way the people did when once they went down with the Lord.

> This was intergen- erational worship. Everyone, including the youngest children and the senior citi- zens, participated.

4   They go on foot down the Mount to the city and all through the city to the Anastasis, but they have to go pretty gently on account of the older women and men among them who might get tired. So it is already late when they reach the Anastasis; but even though it is late they hold Lucernare when they get there, then have a prayer at the Cross, and the people are dismissed.

35

1   Thursday is like the other days from cock-crow till morning in the Anastasis, at nine o'clock, and at midday. But it is the custom to assemble earlier than on ordinary days in the afternoon at the Martyrium, in fact at two o'clock, since the dismissal has to take place sooner. The assembled people have the service. On that day the Offering is made in the Martyrium, and the dismissal takes place at about four in the afternoon. Before the dis- missal the archdeacon makes this announcement: "Let us meet tonight at seven o'clock in the church on the Eleona. There is great effort ahead of us tonight!"

> This Thursday is commonly known as Maundy Thursday.

2   After the dismissal at the Martyrium they go behind the Cross, where they have one hymn and a prayer. Then the bishop makes the Offering there, and everyone receives Commu-

nion. On this one day the Offering is made behind the Cross, but on no other day in the whole year. After the dismissal there they go to the Anastasis, where they have a prayer, the usual blessings of catechumens and faithful, and the dismissal.

Then everybody hurries home for a meal, so that, as soon as they have finished it, they can go to the church on Eleona which contains the cave which on this very day the Lord visited with the apostles.

3   There they continue to sing hymns and antiphons suitable to the place and the day, with readings and prayers between, until about eleven o'clock at night. They read the passages from the Gospel about what the Lord said to his disciples when he sat in the very cave which is in the church.

4   At about midnight they leave and go up with hymns to the Imbomon, the place from which the Lord ascended into heaven. And there they again have readings and hymns and antiphons suitable to the day, and the prayers which the bishop says are all appropriate to the day and the place.

36

Having the advantage of a record of the actual sites in the Gospel accounts of Jesus' passion, Jerusalem's worship proceeds by time and place according to these Scriptures. Egeria has in mind Luke 22:41 as identifying the place where Christ prayed.

1   When the cock begins to crow, everyone leaves the Imbomon and comes down with singing to the place where the Lord prayed, as the Gospels describe in the passage which begins, "And he was parted from them about a stone's cast, and prayed." The bishop and all the people go into a graceful church which has been built there, have a prayer appropriate to the place and the day, and one suitable hymn. Then the Gospel passage is read where Jesus said to his disciples, "Watch, lest ye enter into temptation," and, when the whole passage has been read, there is another prayer.

2   From there all of them, including the smallest children, now go down with singing and conduct the bishop to Gethsemane. There are a great many people, and they have been crowded together, tired by their vigil, and weakened by their daily fasting—and they have had a very big hill to come down—so they go very slowly on their way to Gethsemane. So that they can all see, they are provided with hundreds of church candles.

The loudness of the people's reaction to the account of Jesus' arrest is another reminder of how demonstrative late patristic worship could be. Congregations were not quiet and passive at this time.

3   When everyone arrives at Gethsemane, they have an appropriate prayer, a hymn, and then a reading from the Gospel about the Lord's arrest. By the time it has been read, everyone is groaning and lamenting and weeping so loud that people even across in the city can probably hear it all.

Next they go with singing to the city. They reach the gate at the time when people can first recognize each other. And from there every single one of them, old and young, rich and poor, goes on through the center of the city to be present at the next service—for this above all others is the day when no one leaves the vigil till morning comes. Thus the bishop is conducted from Gethsemane to the gate, and from there through the whole city as far as the Cross.

4 By the time they arrive before the Cross it is pretty well a full day, and they have another Gospel reading, the whole passage about the Lord being led away to Pilate, and all the recorded words of Pilate to the Lord or to the Jews.

5 Then the bishop speaks a word of encouragement to the people. They have been hard at it all night, and there is further effort in store for them in the day ahead. So he tells them not to be weary, but to put their hope in God, who will give them a reward out of all proportion to the effort they have made. When he has given them as much encouragement as he can, he speaks to them as follows: "Now go home till the next service, and sit down for a bit. Then be back here at about eight o'clock so that till midday you can see the holy wood of the Cross, that, as every one of us believes, helps us attain salvation. And from midday onwards we must assemble here before the Cross again and give our minds to readings and prayers till nightfall."

This day that commemorates the death of Christ is often known as Good Friday.

37

1 Before the sun is up, the dismissal takes place at the Cross, and those with the energy then go to Sion to pray at the column at which the Lord was scourged, before going on home for a short rest. But it is not long before everyone is assembled for the next service. The bishop's chair is placed on Golgotha behind the Cross (the cross there now), and he takes his seat. A table is placed before him with a cloth on it. The deacons stand round. There is brought to him a gold and silver box containing the holy wood of the Cross. It is opened, and the wood of the Cross and the title are taken out and placed on the table.

2 As long as the holy wood is on the table, the bishop sits with his hands resting on either end of it and holds it down, and the deacons round him keep watch over it. They guard it like this because what happens now is that all the people, catechumens as well as faithful, come up one by one to the table. They stoop down over it, kiss the wood, and move on. But on one occasion (I don't know when) one of them bit off a piece of the holy wood and stole it away. For this reason the deacons stand round and keep watch in case anyone dares to do the same again.

3 Thus all the people go past one by one. They stoop down, touch the holy wood first with their forehead and then with their eyes, and then kiss it, but no one puts out his hand to touch it. Then they go on to a deacon who stands holding the Ring of Solomon and the Horn with which the kings were anointed. These they venerate by kissing them, and they start round about eight o'clock with everybody going by, entering by one door and going out through the other, till midday. All this takes place where on the previous day, Thursday, they made the offering.

4 At midday they go before the Cross—whether it is rain or shine, for the place is out of doors—into the very spacious and beautiful courtyard between the Cross and the Anastasis, and there is not even room to open a door, the place is so crammed with people.

Egeria shows the steps taken to protect the cross. With the growth of attachment to historic places seems to have come a growth in the attachment to historic objects and the veneration thereof as part of worship. This trend will increase in centuries to come. Of course, Christ's cross, reportedly found by Constantine's mother, Helena, would be the most important object.

The title referred to here is presumably the identification of Christ, which Pontius Pilate ordered to be placed on the cross. See John 19:19.

Notice the coordination between historic places and extensive commemorative Scripture readings as the basis of worship. Jerusalem's worship was focused on God's saving activity in Jesus Christ.

5   They place the bishop's chair before the Cross, and the whole time between midday and three o'clock is taken up with readings. They are all about the things Jesus suffered: first the psalms on this subject, then the Apostles (the Epistles or Acts) which concern it, then passages from the Gospels. Thus they read the prophecies about what the Lord would suffer, and the Gospels about what he did suffer.

6   And in this way they continue the readings and hymns from midday till three o'clock, demonstrating to all the people by the testimony of the Gospels and the writings of the Apostles that the Lord actually suffered everything the prophets had foretold. For those three hours, then, they are teaching the people that nothing which took place had not been foretold, and all that was foretold was completely fulfilled. Between all the readings are prayers, all of them appropriate to the day.

7   It is impressive to see the way all the people are moved by these readings, and how they mourn. You could hardly believe how every single one of them weeps during the three hours, old and young alike, because of the manner in which the Lord suffered for us. Then, when three o'clock comes, they have the reading from St. John's Gospel about Jesus giving up the ghost, and, when that has been read, there is a prayer, and the dismissal.

8   After the dismissal before the Cross, they go directly into the Great Church, the Martyrium, and do what is usual during this week between three o'clock and evening. After the dismissal they leave the Martyrium for the Anastasis, where, once inside, they read the Gospel passage about Joseph asking Pilate for the Lord's body and placing it in a new tomb. After the reading there is a prayer, the blessings of the catechumens and faithful, and the dismissal.

9   On this day there is no announcement that people are to keep vigil in the Anastasis. Obviously they are tired. But nonetheless it is the custom to watch there, and all who wish—I should have said, all who can—keep the vigil there. Some cannot watch till morning, and they do not stay, but the vigil is kept by the clergy, or at any rate by the ones young enough to have the energy. All the night through they sing hymns and antiphons till morning comes. Most of the people watch, but some only come later on, and some at midnight, doing whatever they can manage.

38

The paschal vigil refers to a service that remembers Christ's crucifixion and resurrection. *Pascha* is an ancient term for the passing over of Jesus from death to life.

1   The following day is the Saturday, and they have normal services at nine o'clock and midday. But at three they stop keeping Saturday because they are preparing for the **paschal** vigil in the Great Church, the Martyrium. They keep their paschal vigil like us, but there is one addition. As soon as the "infants" have been baptized and clothed, and left the font, they are led with the bishop straight to the Anastasis.

2   The bishop goes inside the railed area and after one hymn says a prayer for them. Then

he returns with them to the church, where all the people are keeping the vigil in the usual way.

They do all the things to which we are accustomed, and, when the Offering has been made, they have the dismissal. After their dismissal in the Great Church, they at once go with singing to the Anastasis, where the resurrection Gospel is read, and once more the bishop makes the Offering. They waste no time during these services, so as not to detain the people too long; in fact they are dismissed from their vigil at the same time as us.

39

1   The eight days of Easter they celebrate till a late hour, like us, and up to the eighth day of Easter they follow the same order as people do everywhere else. The arrangements and decorations for the eight days of Easter are like those for the season of Epiphany in the Great Church, and also in the Anastasis, at the Cross, on the Eleona, at Bethlehem, the Lazarium, and elsewhere.

2   On the first Sunday, Easter Day itself, they assemble in the Great Church, the Martyrium, and similarly on the Monday and Tuesday; and when they have had the dismissal there, they always go with singing from the Martyrium to the Anastasis. But on the Wednesday they assemble on the Eleona, on the Thursday in the Anastasis, on the Friday on Sion, on the Saturday before the Cross, and on the eighth day, the Sunday, they assemble once more in the Great Church, the Martyrium.

3   On each of the eight days of Easter the bishop, with all the clergy, the "infants" who have been baptized, all the **apotactites,** both men and women, and any of the people who wish, go up to the Eleona after their meal (the Eleona contains the cave where Jesus used to teach his disciples) and in that church they have hymns and prayers, and also at the Imbomon (the place from which the Lord ascended into heaven).

4   When the psalms and prayer are finished, they go down with singing to the Anastasis in time for Lucernare. And this happens on each of the eight days; but on a Sunday at Eastertime, after the people have been dismissed from Lucernare at the Anastasis, they all lead the bishop with singing to Sion.

5   When they get there, they have hymns suitable to the day and the place, a prayer, and the Gospel reading which describes the Lord coming to this place on this day, "when the doors were shut"; for this happened in the very place where the church of Sion now stands. That was when one disciple, Thomas, was not present; and when he returned and the disciples told him that they had seen the Lord, he said, "Unless I see I do not believe." After this reading and another prayer, the catechumens are blessed, and the faithful, and everyone goes home late, at about eight at night.

Egeria describes the series of services held daily during the week after Easter. To fill the week after a great feast (called an octave) with worship was a common practice. During this week, the bishop preached to the newly baptized about what they experienced in their baptisms.

For Egeria, *apotactites* appears to be a synonym for monks and nuns.

In commemoration-based worship, Easter provides a logical choice for grouping baptisms of new converts. Resurrection permeates the day. The Scripture readings speak of it. The empty tomb in the Anastasis offers a historical witness to it. And the converts, baptized into new life and joined to the Body of Christ, the Church, provide a living testimony to the resurrection's ongoing power. Text, place, sacrament, and people come together as witnesses to Christ's resurrection.

40

1   On the eighth day of Easter, the Sunday, all the people go up with the bishop immediately after midday to the Eleona. They start in this church, taking their places for a time and having hymns, antiphons, and prayers appropriate to the day and place. Then they go up to the Imbomon and do as on the Eleona. Then the time comes for all the people and apotactites to take the bishop with singing to the Anastasis, and they arrive there for Lucernare at the usual time.

2   Lucernare is held at the Anastasis and at the Cross, and from there all the people, every single one, conduct the bishop with singing to Sion. When they get there, they have hymns (also suitable to the place and day), and again read the Gospel passage about the Lord coming on the eighth day of Easter to the place where the disciples were, and rebuking Thomas for his unbelief. When they have had the whole passage, and a prayer, the catechumens and the faithful are blessed in the usual way, and everybody goes home, as on Easter Sunday, at eight at night.

41

Egeria probably means that regular services can be held on Wednesdays and Fridays, since no one is fasting on those days, as compared to Lent.

From Easter till **Pentecost** (the fiftieth day after) not a single person fasts, even if he is an apotactite. Throughout the season they have the usual services from cock-crow to morning at the Anastasis, and also at midday and Lucernare, assembling on Sundays in the Great Church, the Martyrium, and afterwards going with singing to the Anastasis. No one is fasting on Wednesdays or Fridays, so on those days they assemble on Sion, but in the morning, and the service takes place in the usual way.

43

Worship on Pentecost Sunday remembers both the outpouring of the Holy Spirit and the Lord Jesus' ascension into heaven at their respective sites around the city.

1   The Fiftieth Day is a Sunday and a great effort for the people. At cock-crow they have the usual service, a vigil service at the Anastasis with the bishop reading the regular Sunday Gospel about the Lord's resurrection. What follows in the Anastasis is what they do during the rest of the year.

2   In the morning the people all assemble in their usual way in the Great Church, the Martyrium, and have sermons from the presbyters and then the bishop. The offering is duly made in the way which is usual on a Sunday, except that the dismissal at the Martyrium is earlier, taking place before nine o'clock, and straight after the dismissal in the Martyrium all the people, every single one, take the bishop with singing to Sion, where they arrive by nine o'clock.

3   When they arrive, they have a reading of the passage from the Acts of the Apostles about the descent of the Spirit and how all the languages spoken were understood, after which the service proceeds as usual.

The presbyters concern themselves with this reading because Sion (though it has now been altered into a church) is the very spot where what I have just mentioned was done by the multitude who were assembled with the apostles after the Lord's passion.

They have the reading there from the Acts of the Apostles, and afterwards the service proceeds as usual, and they make the Offering there. Then as the people are dismissed the archdeacon makes this announcement: "Let us all be ready today on the Mount of Eleona at the Imbomon immediately after midday."

4 So all the people go home for a rest, and as soon as they have had their meal, they go up Eleona, the Mount of Olives, each at his own pace, till there is not a Christian left in the city.

5 Once they have climbed Eleona, the Mount of Olives, they go to the Imbomon (the place from which the Lord ascended into heaven), where the bishop takes his seat, and also the presbyters and all the people. They have readings and between them hymns and antiphons suitable to this day and to the place. Also the prayers which come between are concerned with subjects appropriate to the day and the place. They have the Gospel reading about the Lord's ascension, and then the reading from the Acts of the Apostles about the Lord ascending into heaven after the resurrection.

6 When this is over, the catechumens are blessed, then the faithful.
It is already three o'clock, and they go down with singing from there to the other church on Eleona, containing the cave where the Lord used to sit and teach the apostles. By the time they get there it is after four, and they have Lucernare. The prayer is said, the catechumens are blessed, and then the faithful, and they go out.
All the people, every single one of them, go down with their bishop, singing hymns and antiphons suitable to that day, and so, very gradually, they make their way to the Martyrium.

7 Even when they arrive at the city gate, it is already night, and the people have brought hundreds of church lamps to help them. It is quite a way from the gate to the Great Church, the Martyrium, and they arrive there at about eight at night, going very slowly all the way so that the walk does not make the people tired. The great doors which face the market are opened, and the bishop and all the people enter the Martyrium singing. Inside the church they have hymns and a prayer, and the catechumens are blessed, then the faithful. Then they set off once more with singing to the Anastasis.

8 Again in the Anastasis they have hymns and antiphons and a prayer, and the catechumens are blessed, and then the faithful. Then the same is done again at the Cross, and once more every single member of the Christian community conducts the bishop with singing to Sion.

9 On arrival they have suitable readings, psalms and antiphons, a prayer, the blessing of the catechumens and then the faithful, and then the dismissal. After the dismissal everyone goes to kiss the bishop's hand, and at about midnight everybody goes home. Thus this

is a very hard day for them, for they have never stopped all day since they kept the vigil in the Anastasis, and the services have taken so long that it is midnight by the time they are dismissed on Sion, and all go home.

45

1 I feel I should add something about the way they instruct those who are to be baptized at Easter. Names must be given in before the first day of Lent, which means that a presbyter takes down all the names before the start of the eight weeks for which Lent lasts here, as I have told you.

2 Once the priest has all the names, on the second day of Lent at the start of the eight weeks, the bishop's chair is placed in the middle of the Great Church, the Martyrium. The presbyters sit in chairs on either side of him, and all the clergy stand. Then one by one those seeking baptism are brought up, men coming with their fathers and women with their mothers.

3 As they come in one by one, the bishop asks their neighbors questions about them: "Is this person leading a good life? Does he respect his parents? Is he a drunkard or a boaster?" He asks about all the serious human vices.

4 And if his inquiries show him that someone has not committed any of these misdeeds, he himself puts down his name. But if someone is guilty, he is told to go away, and the bishop tells him that he is to amend his ways before he may come to the font. He asks the men and the women the same questions. But it is not too easy for a visitor to come to baptism if he has no witnesses who are acquainted with him.

46

1 Now, ladies and sisters, I want to write something which will save you from thinking all this is done without due explanation. They have here the custom that those who are preparing for baptism during the season of the Lenten fast go to be exorcised by the clergy first thing in the morning, directly after the morning dismissal in the Anastasis. As soon as that has taken place, the bishop's chair is placed in the Great Church, the Martyrium, and all those to be baptized, the men and the women, sit round him in a circle. There is a place where the fathers and mothers stand, and any of the people who want to listen (the faithful, of course) can come in and sit down.

2 However, the catechumens do not come in while the bishop is teaching.

His subject is God's Law. During the forty days he goes through the whole Bible, beginning with Genesis. First, he relates the literal meaning of each passage, and then he interprets its spiritual meaning. He also teaches them at this time all about the resurrection and the faith. And this is called *catechesis.*

3 After five weeks of teaching they receive the Creed, which he explains article by article in

---

Egeria backtracks in the chronological order of her narrative to give some background information on how people were prepared for baptism.

The "fathers" and "mothers" spoken of here are the godparents or sponsors who normally accompanied all candidates for baptism, regardless of age.

Preparing for baptism was an intense experience involving several dimensions, including a regular round of prayer to make sure that evil forces had been broken in the candidate's life. Note, too, the prior examination that reviewed conduct. What are appropriate thresholds to baptism?

Here Egeria describes part of the intensive preparation one received before baptism. This church, like others of the period, seemed concerned that those being baptized be able to hold the Bible together as an intelligible whole and know how the whole testifies to the Gospel of Jesus Christ (the "spiritual meaning"). This ability to know the breadth of the Bible in a Christian way was a key capacity for participating well in worship in this period.

the same way as he explained the Scriptures, first literally and then spiritually. Thus, all the people in these parts are able to follow the Scriptures when they are read in church, since there has been teaching on all the Scriptures from six to nine in the morning all through Lent, three hours of catechesis a day.

4   At ordinary services when the bishop sits and preaches, ladies and sisters, the faithful utter exclamations, but when they come and hear him explaining the catechesis, their exclamations are far louder, God is my witness; and when it is related and interpreted like this they ask questions on each point.

At nine o'clock they are dismissed from catechesis, and the bishop is taken with singing straight to the Anastasis. So the dismissal is at nine, which makes three hours of teaching a day for seven weeks. But in the eighth, known as the Great Week, there is no time for them to have their teaching if they are to carry out all the services I have described.

5   So when seven weeks have gone by, and only the week of Easter remains, the one which people here call the Great Week, the bishop comes early into the Great Church, the Martyrium. His chair is placed at the back of the apse, behind the altar, and one by one the candidates go up to the bishop, men with their fathers and women with their mothers, and repeat the Creed to him.

6   When they have done so, the bishop speaks to them all as follows: "During these seven weeks you have received instruction in the whole biblical Law. You have heard about the faith and the resurrection of the body. You have also learned all you can as catechumens of the content of the Creed. But the teaching about baptism itself is a deeper mystery, and you have not the right to hear it while you remain catechumens. Do not think it will never be explained; you will hear it all during the eight days of Easter after you have baptized. But so long as you are catechumens you cannot be told God's deep mysteries."

47

1   Then Easter comes. During the eight days from Easter Day to the eighth day, after the dismissal has taken place in the church and they have come with singing into the Anastasis (it does not take long to say the prayer and bless the faithful), the bishop stands leaning against the inner railed area in the cave of the Anastasis and interprets all that takes place in baptism.

2   The newly baptized come into the Anastasis, and any of the faithful who wish to hear the Mysteries. While the bishop is teaching, no catechumen comes in, and the doors are kept shut in case any try to enter. The bishop relates what has been done, and interprets it. As he does so, the applause is so loud that it can be heard outside the church. Indeed, the way he expounds the mysteries and interprets them cannot fail to move his hearers.

3   In this province there are some people who know both Greek and Syriac, but others know

In 46.2 when she says "not catechumens," Egeria seems to be speaking about those catechumens who are not immediately preparing for baptism.

The baptismal candidates had been told neither what would be done in their baptisms nor the meaning of it. The week after Easter was spent disclosing these things and connecting them to the biblical story, as Cyril's sermons show.

If Egeria spoke only Latin, she would have needed someone to translate for her. Her observations, then, would be dependent on the accuracy of the translation.

only one or the other. The bishop may know Syriac, but he never uses it. He always speaks in Greek and has a presbyter beside him who translates the Greek into Syriac, so that everyone can understand what he means.

4   Similarly, the lessons read in church have to be read in Greek, but there is always someone in attendance to translate into Syriac so that the people understand. Of course, there are also people here who speak neither Greek nor Syriac, but Latin. But there is no need for them to be discouraged, since some of the brothers or sisters who speak Latin as well as Greek will explain things to them.

Imagine how noisy it might have been with people whispering translations to those sitting near them.

5   And what I admire and value most is that all the hymns and antiphons and readings they have, and all the prayers the bishop says, are always relevant to the day which is being observed and to the place in which they are used. They never fail to be appropriate.

48

Egeria describes briefly the worship held in September, called Encaenia, when the dedication of the Sepulcher complex was remembered. She makes it sound like an important time of pilgrimage. Encaenia's significance can be seen in the giving of an entire week of special worship to it, paralleling Epiphany and Easter. When Egeria visited Jerusalem, she was only fifty years removed from the original dedication.

1   The date when the Church on Golgotha (called the Martyrium) was consecrated to God is called Encaenia, and on the same day the holy church of the Anastasis was also consecrated, the place where the Lord rose again after his passion. The Encaenia of these holy churches is a feast of special magnificence, since it is on the very date when the cross of the Lord was discovered.

2   So they arranged that this day should be observed with all possible joy by making the original dedication of these holy churches coincide with the very day when the cross had been found. You will find in the Bible that the day of Encaenia was when the House of God was consecrated, and Solomon stood in prayer before God's altar, as we read in the Books of Chronicles.

49

1   At the time of Encaenia they keep festival for eight days, and for many days beforehand the crowds begin to assemble. Monks and apotactites come not only from the provinces having large numbers of them, such as Mesopotamia, Syria, Egypt, and the Thebaid, but from every region and province. Not one of them fails to make it to Jerusalem to share the celebrations of this solemn feast. There are also lay men and women from every province gathering in Jerusalem at this time for the holy day.

2   And although bishops are few and far between, they never have less than forty or fifty in Jerusalem at this time, accompanied by many of their clergy. In fact I should say that people regard it as a grave sin to miss taking part in this solemn feast, unless anyone had been prevented from coming by an emergency.

3   The feast ranks with Easter or Epiphany, and during Encaenia they decorate the churches in the same way, and assemble each day in different holy places, as at Easter and Epiphany. On the first and second days they assemble in the Great Church, the Martyrium, on

the third day in the Eleona Church on the Mount from which the Lord ascended into heaven after his passion (I mean the church which contains the cave where the Lord taught the apostles on the Mount of Olives). On the fourth day. . . .

This last line breaks off in mid-sentence because the remaining pages are lost from the manuscript.

Source: The account of Egeria's experience in Jerusalem is drawn from John Wilkinson's book *Egeria's Travels* (London: SPCK, 1971; rev. edition, Warminster: Aris & Phillips Ltd., 1999; 3rd edition), pp.142-64. The critical edition of this travel diary in Latin is Corpus Christianorum: Series Latina, vol. 175 (Turnhout, Belgium: Brepols, 1965), which was based on K. Vretska, *Die Pilgerreise der Aetheria (Peregrinatio Aetheria)* (Klosterneuburg, 1958), and O. Prinz, *Itinerarium Egeriae* (Heidelberg, 1960). The section numbers in Egeria's diary have varied among published editions. The numbers chosen here follow this Latin text. For a different English translation of Egeria's diary, see Lawrence J. Johnson's *Worship in the Early Church: An Anthology of Historical Sources,* vol. 2 (Collegeville, Minn.: Liturgical Press, 2010).

Egeria's diary was originally published in 1887 with a treatise, *On the Mysteries: with three Hymns* as *S.Hilarii Tractatvs de mysteriis et hymni et S. Silviae Aqvitanae Peregrinatio ad loca sancta,* Biblioteca dell' Accademia storico-giuridica, vol. 4 (Romae, ex typographia Pacis P. Cuggiani). It was published by Gian Francesco Gammurrini from the sole surviving manuscript that he found in Arezzo, Italy. A revised edition appeared the following year as fasc. 2°-3° of the *Studi e documenti di storie e diritto,* anno IX. The authorship has since been ascribed to a nun, Aetheria (Etheria, Eucheria, Egeria) mentioned by a Spanish monk, Valerius (7th century) in a letter to the Fratres bergidenses. Cf. Dom Férotin, *Revue des questions historiques,* v. 79 (1903); P. Geyer, *Die wirkliche verfasserin der "Peregrinatio Silviae" in Archiv f. latein.* lexikogr. XV (1908); Teuffel, vol. III (1913); Schanz, vol. IV (1914). The Arezzo manuscript includes the *Tractatus de mysteriis* of Hilarius, followed by three hymns of doubtful authorship, in the manuscript ascribed to Hilarius. The manuscript likely came to Arezzo from the monastery of Monte Cassino when Ambrose Rastrellini came from Monte Cassino to be Abbot at Arezzo, perhaps in 1599. It was translated into Russian in 1888 and was first published with an English translation by J.H. Bernard in 1891.

ORDER OF SERVICE AND TEXTS

The Scripture Readings Likely Used in Jerusalem

The following set of Scripture readings, called a **lectionary**, *reflects Jerusalem's practice approximately fifty years after the period considered in this chapter. However, this lectionary, exported to Armenia in the first half of the fifth century, is the closest depiction of earlier Jerusalem practices regarding the use of the Bible in worship. While development did occur since the time of Cyril and Egeria (and that is reflected here), the core of the lectionary does reveal what Cyril's church would have done. The lectionary indicates the structure of the church year, the stational character of Jerusalem's worship (i.e., its movement from place to place), and the relative weight placed on which biblical books. The numbering of the different sections of the lectionary is that provided in previously published editions. The year begins with Epiphany.*

1. This is the record of the **synaxes** as kept in Jerusalem at the holy places of Christ. It indicates the date of the month, the reading of the day, and the psalm appropriate to the feasts and the memorials. If in this book the same thing is repeated two times, three times, or more, let no one ascribe this action to ignorance, but much rather to our diligence. This is done so that one can find the proper place for each synaxis and reading without difficulty.

   A synaxis is an assembly for liturgical purposes.

   The feast of the Holy Epiphany takes place on January 6.

   The day before Epiphany (January 5) at the Place of the Shepherds, at the tenth hour:
   Psalm 23 (antiphon: v. 1: "The Lord is my shepherd.")
   Alleluia: Psalm 80 (v. 1: "O shepherd of Israel, hear us, you who lead.")
   Gospel: Luke 2:8-20
   Old Testament: Genesis 1:28-3:20
   Old Testament: Isaiah 7:10-17
   Old Testament: Exodus 14:24-15:21
   Old Testament: Micah 5:2-7
   Old Testament: Proverbs 1:2-9
   Old Testament: Isaiah 9:5b-7
   Old Testament: Isaiah 11:1-9
   Old Testament: Isaiah 35:3-8
   Old Testament: Isaiah 40:10-17

   The "tenth hour" refers to the tenth hour of daytime, i.e., approximately 4 P.M.

   The common practice of walking through God's "greatest hits" of the Old Testament was considered the appropriate way to worship during the most important yearly commemorations of Christ's life. Epiphany in Jerusalem remembered Christ's birth as a revealing of God to the nations, using the Gospel of Matthew. Note a similar Old Testament use at Easter.

65

Old Testament: Isaiah 42:1-8a

Old Testament: Daniel 3:1-23 with the Prayer of Azariah and the Song of the Three Jews, 1-12a (Refrain: "Lord, you have made the dew fall, a dew of mercy, and quenched the flame of burning fire, for it is you alone who is recognized as Savior.")

Old Testament: The Prayer of Azariah and the Song of the Three Jews, 12b-28 (Refrain: "You have had pity on our fathers. You have visited us. You have saved us.")

Old Testament: The Prayer of Azariah and the Song of the Three Jews, 29-68.

After they have read the hymn:

Psalm 2 (antiphon: v. 7: "The Lord said to me, 'You are my son; today I have begotten you.'")

Apostle: Titus 2:11-15

Alleluia: Psalm 110 (v. 1: "The Lord said to my Lord, 'Sit at my right hand.'")

Gospel: Matthew 2:1-12

2. **At dawn, at the Holy Martyrium:**

Psalm 2 (antiphon: v. 7: "The Lord said to me, 'You are my son; today I have begotten you.'")

Apostle: Titus 2:11-1

Alleluia: Psalm 110 (v. 1: "The Lord said to my Lord, 'Sit at my right hand.'")

Gospel: Matthew 1:18-25

3. **The second day, at the Martyrium of Saint Stephen:**

Psalm 5 (antiphon: v.12: "Lord, as with a shield, you have crowned us with your favor.")

Apostle: Acts 6:8-8:2

Apostle: Titus 2:11-15

Alleluia: Psalm 21 (v.1: "Lord, we rejoice in your power.")

Gospel: John 12:24-26

4. **The third day, on Sunday, at the Holy Martyrium:**

Psalm 2 (antiphon: v. 7: "The Lord said to me, 'You are my son; today I have begotten you.'")

Apostle: Hebrews 1:1-12

Alleluia: Psalm 110 (v. 1: "The Lord said to my Lord, 'Sit at my right hand.'")

Gospel: Matthew 2:13-23

5. **The fourth day, at Holy Sion:**

Psalm 110 (antiphon: v. 3: "In the splendor of the saints, before the morning star, I have begotten you.")

Apostle: Galatians 4:1-7

The Prayer of Azariah and another passage known as the Song of the Three Jews/Youths/Children are additional texts found after Daniel 3:23 in the Greek Old Testament used in the early church and known as the Septuagint. These materials are omitted from Protestant Bibles as apocryphal additions.

The Martyrium of Saint Stephen was built after the time of Cyril and Egeria. Constructed north of Jerusalem's walls and dedicated in 439, it contained the bones of Stephen, the biblical martyr of Acts 7.

As was typical with major yearly feasts, the week following had special worship services.

Alleluia, Psalm 132 (v. 1: "Lord, do not forget the trials of David.")

Gospel: Luke 1:26-38

6. **The fifth day, at the Holy Mount of Olives:**

Psalm 99 (antiphon: v. 9: "Exalt the Lord our God, adore him on his holy mountain.")

Apostle: Hebrews 12:18-27

Alleluia: Psalm 15 (v. 1: "Lord, who may dwell in your sanctuary?")

Gospel: Luke 1:39-56

7. **The sixth day, at the Lazarium:**

Psalm 30 (antiphon: v. 3: "Lord, you have brought me up from hell, you have saved me from going down into the pit.")

Apostle: 1 Thessalonians 4:13-5:18

Alleluia, Psalm 40 (v. 1: "I waited for the Lord, and he heard my cry.")

Gospel: John 11:1-46

8. **The seventh day, at Holy Golgotha:**

Psalm 96 (antiphon: v. 2: "Announce, from day to day, his salvation.")

Apostle: Romans 1:1-7

Alleluia: Psalm 72 (v.1: "God, give the king your justice.")

Gospel: Luke 2:1-7

9. **The eighth day, the day of the Circumcision of our Savior Jesus Christ, at the Holy Anastasis:**

Psalm 98 (antiphon: v. 2: "The Lord has shown his salvation, before the nations he has revealed his justice.")

Apostle: Colossians 2:8-15

Alleluia: Psalm 85 (v. 1: "You favored your land and restored to Jacob his benevolence.")

Gospel: Luke 2:21

The scriptures for the synaxes of the Holy Epiphany are now finished.

10. **Commemoration of Peter and Absalom (January 11):**

Psalm 116:10-19 (antiphon: v. 15: "Precious in the sight of the Lord is the death of his saints.")

Apostle: Romans 8:28-39

And then the acts of their martyrdom are recounted.

Alleluia: Psalm 116:1-9 (v. 1: "I love the Lord, for he heard my cry.")

Gospel: Matthew 10:16-22

11. **Commemoration of Saint Anthony, Hermit (January 17), at the Holy Anastasis:**

Psalm 116:10-19 (antiphon: v. 15: "Precious in the sight of the Lord is the death of his saints.")

Apostle: Hebrews 11:32-40

Alleluia: Psalm 116:1-9 (v. 1: "I love the Lord, for he heard my cry.")

Gospel: Matthew 10:37-42

12. **Commemoration of the Great King Theodosius (January 19) at the Holy Anastasis:**

Psalm 132 (antiphon: v. 1: "Lord, do not forget the trials of David.")

Apostle: 1 Timothy 2:1-7

Alleluia: Psalm 21 (v. 1: "Lord, we rejoice in your power.")

Gospel: Luke 7:1-10

One must think holistically with the Gospel of Christ at the center to understand the logic of these early lectionary selections. A reading is not an isolated event, but a witness to what God has done in Jesus Christ. On this occasion the texts work together to proclaim that God has revealed salvation to the whole world through Christ.

13. **Commemoration of the fortieth day of the Nativity of our Lord Jesus Christ (February 14), in the Holy Martyrium:**

Psalm 98 (antiphon: v. 3: "All the ends of the earth have seen the salvation of our God.")

Apostle: Galatians 3:24-29

Alleluia: Psalm 96 (v. 1: "Sing to the Lord a new song, sing to the Lord.")

Gospel: Luke 2:22-40

14. **Commemoration of the Forty Saints (March 9) at the Martyrium of Saint Stephen:**

The same scripture used for the other saints is carried out, and the acts of their martyrdom are recited.

The inclusion of Cyril in this lectionary is a clue that it comes from a time after his episcopacy.

15. **Commemoration of Cyril, Bishop of Jerusalem (March 18):**

Psalm 116:10-19 (antiphon: v. 15: "Precious in the sight of the Lord is the death of his saints.")

Apostle: 2 Timothy 4:1-8

Alleluia: Psalm 116:1-9 (v. 1: "I love the Lord, for he heard my cry.")

Gospel: John 10:11-16

16. **Commemoration of John, Bishop of Jerusalem (March 29):**

The same scripture is performed as for the commemoration of Cyril.

17. **Instruction for those who are written in the book for the Holy Fast, and who are preparing to receive baptism:**

Old Testament: Isaiah 1:16-20

Old Testament: Ezekiel 18:20b-23

Apostle: Romans 6:3-14

Apostle: Colossians 2:8-3:4

Apostle: Hebrews 11:1-31

Old Testament: Isaiah 45:16b-25

Apostle: Ephesians 3:14-4:13

Old Testament: Jeremiah 32: 18b-44*

Old Testament: Job 38:2-40:5

Apostle: 1 Corinthians 8:5-9:23

Apostle: Hebrews 1:1-2:1

Old Testament: Isaiah 7:10-8:10

Old Testament: Isaiah 53:1-54:5

Apostle: 1 Corinthians 15:1-28

Old Testament: Daniel 7:2-27

Apostle: 1 Corinthians 12:1-7

Apostle: 1 Corinthians 12:8-27

Old Testament: Ezekiel 37:1-14

Apostle: 1 Timothy 3:14-16

Although difficult to coordinate exactly with what is found in Cyril's existing Lenten catechesis, the readings here offer some of the critical passages considered important to know to prepare for baptism. Notice what it prioritizes. It begins with readings about forgiveness, faith, and piety. Then the readings move like a creed from creation in Job 38 through the life of Christ and the church to re-creation with the dry bones in Ezekiel.

18. **The first week of Lent, on Wednesday, at the tenth hour, at Holy Sion:**

Old Testament: Exodus 1:1-2:10

Old Testament: Joel 1:14-20

Psalm 51 (antiphon: v. 1: "Have pity on me, God, according to your great mercy; according to the abundance of your compassion erase my iniquities.")

19. **The first week of Lent, on Friday, at the tenth hour, at Holy Sion:**

Old Testament: Deuteronomy 6:4-7:10

Old Testament: Job 6:2-7:13

Old Testament: Isaiah 40:1-8

Psalm 41 (antiphon: v. 4: "I said, 'Lord have mercy on me, heal my soul; I have sinned against you.'")

Note the greater use of Old Testament texts during these weekday services in Lent compared to the readings for Sundays in other times of the year. In this way the Jerusalem church gets a diet of Scripture from across the whole Bible over the course of a year.

20. **The second week of Lent, on Monday, at the tenth hour, at the Holy Anastasis:**

Old Testament: 1 Samuel 1:1-23a

Old Testament: Proverbs 1:2-33

Old Testament: Jeremiah 1:1-10

Psalm 130 (antiphon: v. 2: "Let your ears be attentive to the voice of my prayer.")

* Renoux lists this as 39:19b-44, and Wilkinson has it as 32:19b-44.

21. **On Tuesday, at the tenth hour, at the Holy Anastasis:**

    Old Testament: 1 Samuel 1:23b-2:26

    Old Testament: Proverbs 2:1-3:10

    Old Testament: Jeremiah 1:11-2:3

    Psalm 27 (antiphon: v. 7: "Lord, hear my voice, for I cry to you; have mercy on me and hear me.")

22. **On Wednesday, at the tenth hour, at Holy Sion:**

    Old Testament: Exodus 2:11-22

    Old Testament: Joel 2:1-11

    Old Testament: Micah 4:1-7

    Psalm 57 (antiphon: v. 1a: "Have mercy on me, God, have mercy on me; for in you has my soul trusted.")

23. **On Thursday, at the tenth hour, at the Holy Anastasis:**

    Old Testament: 1 Samuel 3:2-4:18

    Old Testament: Proverbs 3:11-4:14

    Old Testament: Jeremiah 2:31-3:16

    Psalm 39 (antiphon: v. 12: "Hear my prayer, Lord; give ear to my supplications.")

24. **On Friday, at the tenth hour, at Holy Sion:**

    Old Testament: Deuteronomy 7:11-8:1

    Old Testament: Job 9:2-10:2a

    Old Testament: Isaiah 40:9-17

    Psalm 65 (antiphon: v. 5: "Hear us, God our Savior, Hope of all the ends of the earth.")

25. **The third week of Lent, on Wednesday, at the tenth hour, at Holy Sion:**

    Old Testament: Exodus 2:23-3:15

    Old Testament: Joel 2:21-32

    Psalm 71:1 (antiphon: v. 1: "In you, Lord, have I hoped; let me never be put to shame.")

26. **On Friday, at the tenth hour, at Holy Sion:**

    Old Testament: Deuteronomy 8:11-9:10

    Old Testament: Job 12:2-13:6

    Old Testament: Isaiah 42:1-8a

    Psalm 75 (antiphon: v. 1: "We praise you, God; we praise you and call upon your holy name.")

27. **The fourth week of Lent, on Wednesday at the tenth hour, at Holy Sion:**

    Old Testament: Exodus 3:16-22

    Old Testament: Joel 3:1-8

    Psalm 77 (antiphon: v. 1: "With my voice I cried to the Lord; with my voice I cried to God, and he set his eyes upon me.")

28. **On Friday, at the tenth hour, at Holy Sion:**

    Old Testament: Deuteronomy 9:11-24

    Old Testament: Job 16:2-17:16

    Old Testament: Isaiah 43:22-44:8

    Psalm 83 (antiphon: v. 18: "Let them know that your name is the Lord, and that you alone are the Most High over all the earth.")

29. **The fifth week of Lent, on Wednesday at the tenth hour, at Holy Sion:**

    Old Testament: Exodus 4:1-21a

    Old Testament: Joel 3:9-21

    Psalm 84 (antiphon: v. 4: "Blessed are those who dwell in the house of the Lord; to the ages of the ages they praise you.")

30. **On Friday, at the tenth hour, at Holy Sion:**

    Old Testament: Deuteronomy 10:1-15

    Old Testament: Job 19:2-29

    Old Testament: Isaiah 45:1-13

    Psalm 85 (antiphon: v. 7: "Show us, Lord, your mercy, and grant us your salvation.")

31. **The sixth week of Lent, on Wednesday at the tenth hour, at Holy Sion:**

    Old Testament: Exodus 4:21-5:3

    Old Testament: Zechariah 9:9-16a

    Psalm 86 (antiphon: vv. 15-16: "Patient [Lord], full of mercy, and true, turn to me and have pity.")

32. **On Friday, at the tenth hour, at Holy Sion:**

    Old Testament: Deuteronomy 11:10-25

    Old Testament: Job 21:2-34

    Old Testament: Isaiah 46:3-47:4

    Psalm 88 (antiphon: v. 2: "Let my prayer come before you, Lord; incline your ear to my supplication.")

33. **On the sixth day before the Passover of the Law, on Saturday, at the tenth hour, at the Lazarium:**

Psalm 30 (antiphon: v. 3: "Lord, you have brought up my soul from hell, and you have saved me from those who go down into the Pit.")

Apostle: 1 Thessalonians 4:13-18

Alleluia: Psalm 40 (v. 1: "I waited for the Lord, and he heard my cry.")

Gospel: John 11:55-12:11

34. **On Sunday, the Day of Palms, at the Holy Martyrium:**

Psalm 98 (antiphon: vv. 8-9: "Let the mountains exult before the Lord, for the Lord is coming and he arrives to judge.")

Apostle: Ephesians 1:3-10

Alleluia: Psalm 97 (v. 1: "The Lord reigns; let the earth be exalted.")

Gospel: Matthew 20:29-21:17

The same day, at the ninth hour, they ascend the Mount of Olives with the branches of palm trees, and there they sing songs and pray until about the eleventh hour. Then they descend together to the Holy Anastasis while singing:

Psalm 118 (antiphon: v. 26: "Blessed is he who comes in the name of the Lord! Blessed is he who comes!")

35. **On the Monday of Holy Week, at the tenth hour, at the Holy Martyrium:**

Old Testament: Genesis 1:1-3:24

Old Testament: Proverbs 1:2-9

Old Testament: Isaiah 40:1-8

Psalm 65 (antiphon: v. 5: "Hear us, God our Savior, Hope of all the ends of the earth.")

36. **On Tuesday, at the tenth hour, on the Mount of Olives:**

Old Testament: Genesis 6:9-9:17

Old Testament: Proverbs 9:1-11

Old Testament: Isaiah 40:9-17

Psalm 25 (antiphon: vv. 1-2: "To you, Lord, have I lifted my soul; in you, God, I have placed my hope that I will never be confounded.")

37. **On Wednesday, at the tenth hour, at the Holy Martyrium:**

Old Testament: Genesis 18:1-19:30

Old Testament: Proverbs 1:10-19

Old Testament: Zechariah 11:11-14

Psalm 41 (antiphon: v. 4: "I said, 'Lord, have mercy on me: heal my soul, for I have sinned against you.'")

And after the psalm, they immediately descend to the Holy Anastasis and read the Gospel according to Matthew 26:3-16.

38. On the Thursday of Holy Week, concerning which Jesus said to his disciples, "I ardently desire to eat this Passover with you," they gather at the beginning of the seventh hour, at the Holy Martyrium:

Old Testament: Genesis 22:1-18

Old Testament: Isaiah 61:1-6

Apostle: Acts 1:15-26

Psalm 55 (antiphon: v. 21: "His words are smoother than oil, and yet they are like darts.")

After the psalm, they sit for the homily, and the catechumens are dismissed.

39. And after the dismissal of the catechumens, they gather again:

Psalm 23 (antiphon: v. 5: "You have prepared a table before me, in the sight of my oppressors.")

Apostle: 1 Corinthians 11:23-32

Gospel: Matthew 26:17-20

Then the sacrifice is offered in the Holy Martyrium and before the Holy Cross.

And they immediately go to Holy Sion:

Psalm 23 (antiphon: v. 5: "You have prepared a table before me, in the sight of my oppressors.")

Apostle: 1 Corinthians 11:23-32

Gospel: Mark 14:1-26

They immediately ascend the Mount of Olives, and they do the evening **office** and the vigil.

At the Mount of Olives, they pray groups of psalms on bended knee.

Psalms 2, 3, and 4 (antiphon: 2:2b: "The princes of the peoples have gathered together against the Lord and against his Christ.")

Psalms 40, 41, and 42 (antiphon: 41:7a, 38:21a: "They have set an unjust word against me; Lord, Lord, do not abandon me!")

The catechumens are dismissed before the readings of Scripture that deal with the Lord's Supper. This exclusion is consistent with common practice across Christianity at the time to restrict unbaptized persons' knowledge of the sacrament. Also, notice the use of Psalm 23 to interpret the meaning of Communion.

The office refers to prayer services, normally held on a daily basis and without sermon or sacrament.

After the commemoration of the Last Supper, the Jerusalem church began its detailed worship "walk-through" of the events surrounding the passion, burial, and resurrection of Jesus Christ. It is almost as if it had a three-day-long service, interrupted only by some intermissions.

Psalms 58, 59, and 60 (antiphon: 59:1: "God, deliver me from my enemies, and save me from my persecutors.")

Psalms 78, 79, and 80 (antiphon: 88:5c, 79:13a: "They are expelled from your hand; we are your people, and the sheep of your pasture.")

Psalms 108, 109, and 110 (antiphon: 109:2b-3a: "They have spoken against me with a lying tongue, and have surrounded me with words of hate.")

And after the fifteen psalms in the five groupings and the five prayers, in the same evening at midnight:

Gospel: John 13:16-18:1

40. At the same hour of the night, on the Mountain, at the Summit:

Psalm 109 (antiphon: v. 4: "Instead of loving me, they betrayed me, and I continued to pray.")

Gospel: Luke 22:1-65

At the same hour of the night, they gather at the Room of the Disciples:

Gospel: Mark 14:27-72

At the same hour of the night, they descend the Holy Mount of Olives to Gethsemane:

Gospel: Matthew 26:31-56.

41. Following this, they go, singing psalms, to the Courtyard of the House of the High Priest Caiaphas, at the Place of the Repentance of Peter:

Gospel: Matthew 26:57-75

42. At the same hour of the night:

Psalm 118 (antiphon: v. 1: "Give glory to the Lord, for he is good, and his mercy is forever.")

And beginning at the gate, they begin singing psalms until they arrive before Holy Golgotha:

Psalms 78, 79, and 80 (antiphon: 88:5c, 79:13a: "They are expelled from your hand; we are your people, and the sheep of your pasture.")

At Holy Golgotha:

Gospel: John 18:2-27

Although any one of a number of examples could be given, this instance shows how the church coordinated assembling at a given locale according to the scriptural account and using Old and New Testament material "appropriate for the time and place."

At dawn:

Psalm 109 (antiphon: v. 4: "Instead of loving me, they betrayed me, and I continued to pray.")

Gospel: John 18:28-19:16a

43. **On Friday morning of Holy Week, the precious wood of the Cross is placed before Holy Golgotha. And those who are assembled adore it, offering adoration until the sixth hour. And at the sixth hour, they gather at Holy Golgotha, and they say eight Psalms, do eight readings from the Prophets, eight from the Apostles, and for each Psalm, two readings, and one prayer only:**

Psalm 35 (antiphon: v. 11: "Unjust witnesses stood, asking things I do not know.")

Old Testament: Zechariah 11:11-14

Apostle: Galatians 6:14-18

Prayer

Psalm 38 (antiphon: v. 17: "I am ready for torments, and my sorrows are always before me.")

Old Testament: Isaiah 3:9b-15

Apostle: Philippians 2:5-11

Prayer

Psalm 41 (antiphon: v. 6b: "In his heart, he gathered iniquity to himself.")

Old Testament: Isaiah 50:4-9a

Apostle: Romans 5:6-11

Prayer

Psalm 22 (antiphon: v. 18: "They parted my garments among them, and cast lots for my robe.")

Old Testament: Amos 8:9-12

Apostle: 1 Corinthians 1:18-31

Prayer

Psalm 31 (antiphon: v. 5: "Into your hands I commit my spirit.")

Old Testament: Isaiah 52:13-53:12

Apostle: Hebrews 2:11-18

Gospel: Matthew 27:1-56

Prayer

The Scriptures used to mark the time of Jesus' crucifixion on Good Friday span a range: Worshipers in Jerusalem hear prophecies announcing the death of the Savior, the apostle Paul's interpretation of the significance of this death, as well as the Gospel accounts of the passion. Once again this church takes a whole-Bible approach to God's saving activity in Christ.

Psalm 69 (antiphon: v. 21: "They gave me gall for food, and in my thirst gave me vinegar to drink.")

Old Testament: Isaiah 63:1-6

Apostle: Hebrews 9:11-28

Gospel: Mark 15:1-41

Prayer

Psalm 88 (antiphon: vv. 4b-5a: "I became like a man without help, and free among the dead.")

Old Testament: Jeremiah 11:18-20

Apostle: Hebrews 10:19-31

Gospel: Luke 22:66-23:49

Prayer

Psalm 102 (antiphon: v. 1: "Lord, hear my prayer; let my cry come to you.")

Old Testament: Zechariah 14:5c-11

Apostle: 1 Timothy 6:13-16

Gospel: John 19:16b-37

Prayer

After the reading of the Gospel, at the tenth hour, they immediately enter the Holy Martyrium:

Old Testament: Jeremiah 11:18-12:8

Old Testament: Isaiah 53:1-12

Psalm 22 (antiphon: v. 18: "They parted my garments among them, and cast lots for my robe.")

After the Psalm, they immediately descend to the Holy Anastasis:

Gospel: Matthew 27:57-61

44. On Saturday morning, in the Holy Anastasis:

Psalm 88 (antiphon: v. 6: "They laid me in the deepest pit, in the darkness, and in the shadows.")

Gospel: Matthew 27:62-66

On Saturday evening, in the Holy Passover, the bishop sings songs in the Holy Anastasis:

Psalm 113 (antiphon: v. 2: "May the name of the Lord be blessed, now and forever.")

And in the same hour, they ascend to the Holy Martyrium, and the bishop lights a lamp.

As with Epiphany, worshipers held a worship vigil by walking through important Old Testament scriptures to lead the way to celebrating the resurrection. Thus, the whole Bible was held together as a single story of salvation by one God.

And the clergy immediately begin the vigil of the Holy Passover, and they do twelve readings. And for each reading, the prayer is done with kneeling:

Psalm 118 (antiphon: v. 24: "This is the day that the Lord has made. Exult and rejoice in it!")

Old Testament: Genesis 1:1-3:24

Prayer with kneeling

Old Testament: Genesis 22:1-18

Prayer with kneeling

Old Testament: Exodus 12:1-24

Prayer with kneeling

Old Testament: Jonah 1:1-4:11

Prayer with kneeling

Old Testament: Exodus 14:24-15:21 (antiphon: 15:21b: "Let us sing to the Lord, for he is covered in glory!")

Prayer with kneeling

Old Testament: Isaiah 60:1-13

Prayer with kneeling

Old Testament: Job 38:2-28

Prayer with kneeling

Old Testament: 2 Kings 2:1-22

Prayer with kneeling

Old Testament: Jeremiah 31:31-34

Prayer with kneeling

Old Testament: Joshua 1:1-9

Prayer with kneeling

Old Testament: Ezekiel 37:1-14

Prayer with kneeling

Old Testament: Daniel 3:1-23 with the Prayer of Azariah and the Song of the Three Jews,
1-12a (Refrain: "Lord, you have made the dew fall, a dew of mercy, and quenched the
flame of burning fire, for it is you alone who is recognized as Savior.")

Old Testament: The Prayer of Azariah and the Song of the Three Jews, 12b-28
(Refrain: "You have had pity on our fathers. You have visited us. You have saved us.")

Old Testament: The Prayer of Azariah and the Song of the Three Jews, 29-68.

And while they sing the hymn, at midnight, a great number of the newly baptized enter
with the bishop:

Psalm 65 (antiphon: v. 1: "To you, God, belongs the praise in Sion, and to you is presented
prayer in Jerusalem!")

Apostle: 1 Corinthians 15:1-11

Alleluia: Psalm 30 (v. 1: "I will exalt you, O God, for you lifted me up from the depths.")

Gospel: Matthew 28:1-20

And at the same hour, the sacrifice is offered. And after the dismissal, at the same hour of
the night, it is offered at the Holy Anastasis, in front of Holy Golgotha. And immediately they read at the Holy Anastasis:

Gospel: John 19:38-20:18

45. **Easter Sunday, at the Holy Martyrium:**

Psalm 65 (antiphon: v. 1: "To you, God, belongs the praise in Sion, and to you is presented
prayer in Jerusalem!")

Apostle: Acts 1:1-14

Alleluia: Psalm 147:12-20 (v. 12: "Jerusalem, praise the Lord and bless your God!")

Gospel: Mark 15:42-16:8

On the same Easter Sunday, at the ninth hour, they ascend the Holy Mount of Olives. Here
they sing psalms for a little while. They descend, singing psalms, to Holy Anastasis,
and from there in the evening they go to Holy Sion:

Psalm 149 (antiphon: v. 1: "Sing to the Lord a new song, praise for him in the assembly of
the saints!")

Gospel: John 20:19-25

46. **On Monday, in the Holy Martyrium:**

Psalm 65 (antiphon: v. 1: "To you, God, belongs the praise in Sion.")

Apostle: Acts 2:22-41

Alleluia: Psalm 147:12-20 (v. 12: "Jerusalem, praise the Lord and bless your God!")

Gospel: Luke 23:50-24:12

The Scriptures read and the arrival of the newly baptized provided a dual witness to the resurrecting power of God through Jesus Christ.

Another week of glorious worship celebration follows Easter. In these services the bishop would have preached on the meaning of the sacraments to the newly baptized.

47. On Tuesday, at the Holy Martyrium of the first biblical martyr Stephen:

Psalm 5 (antiphon: v. 12: "Lord, as with a shield, you have crowned us with your favor.")

Apostle: Acts 2:42-3:21

Alleluia: Psalm 21 (v. 1: "Lord, in your power we rejoice.")

Gospel: Luke 24:13-35

48. On Wednesday, at Holy Sion:

Psalm 147 (antiphon: v. 12: "Jerusalem, praise the Lord and bless your God!")

Apostle: Acts 3:22-4:12

Apostle: James 1:1-12

Alleluia: Psalm 65 (v. 1: "Praise awaits you in Sion, O God.")

Gospel: Luke 24:36-40

49. On Thursday, on the Holy Mount of Olives:

Psalm 99 (antiphon: v. 9: "Exalt the Lord our God, adore him on the mountain.")

Apostle: Acts 4:13-31

Apostle: James 1:13-27

Alleluia: Psalm 15 (v. 1: "Lord, who may dwell in your sanctuary?")

Gospel: Matthew 5:1-12

50. On Friday, before Holy Golgotha:

Psalm 98 (antiphon: v. 3b: "All the ends of the earth have seen the salvation of our God!")

Apostle: Acts 4:32-5:11

Apostle: James 2:1-13

Alleluia: Psalm 93 (v. 1: "The Lord reigns in majesty.")

Gospel: John 21:1-14

51. On Saturday, at the Holy Anastasis:

Psalm 67 (antiphon: v. 1a: "Our God, have mercy on us and bless us.")

Apostle: Acts 5:12-33

Apostle: James 2:14-26

Alleluia: Psalm 81 (v. 1: "Joyfully exult in God! 'He is our Help,' cry out!")

Gospel: John 21:15-25

In the week following Easter, the Jerusalem church overflows with praise, as evidenced by the joyful quality of the Psalms during the week. The emotional quality contrasts sharply with that of Lent.

52. On Sunday, at the Holy Martyrium:

Psalm 65 (antiphon: v. 1: "To you, God, belongs the praise in Sion.")

Apostle: Acts 5:34-6:7

Apostle: James 3:1-13

Alleluia: Psalm 147:12-20 (v. 12: "Jerusalem, praise the Lord and bless your God!")

Gospel: John 1:1-17

The same Sunday, at the tenth hour, they ascend the Mount of Olives and sing psalms for a little while. They descend, singing songs, to the Holy Anastasis. And from there, in the evening, they go to Holy Sion:

Psalm 149 (antiphon: v. 1: "Sing to the Lord a new song, praise for him in the assembly of the saints!")

Gospel: John 20:26-31

The bishop, accompanied by the ministers, takes those who are newly baptized and enters the Holy Anastasis. Here they hear the mysteries read and the preaching during the week after Easter.

On the second day:

Apostle: 1 Peter 5:8-14

On the sixth day:

Apostle: 1 John 2:20-27

On the seventh day:

Apostle: 1 Corinthians 11:23-32

On the Sunday after Easter:

Apostle: 1 Peter 2:1-10

53. **Commemoration of the Prophet Jeremiah (May 1), at Anathoth, a pilgrimage site close to Jerusalem:**

Psalm 30 (antiphon: v. 3: "He has brought me up out of the pit of misery, out of the mud and the filth.")

Old Testament: Jeremiah 1:1-10

Old Testament: Jeremiah 38:1-13

Apostle: 2 Peter 2:9-22

Alleluia: Psalm 30 (v. 1: "I exalt you, Lord, for you have healed me.")

Gospel: Matthew 2:16-18

The "**mystagogical** readings" are those Scripture texts used by the bishop in explaining the meaning of the sacraments to the newly baptized.

These Scriptures for the days of the week after Easter are texts for preaching to the newly baptized to disclose the meaning of what they had just experienced in their Easter baptisms. The provision of only four texts is one of those frustrating points for historians, since Cyril and Egeria both said that the preaching took place every day during this week, and another manuscript of this lectionary provides an additional reading. Compounding the difficulty is that only five of these types of sermons have been attributed to Cyril. Such discrepancies mean that reconstructions or descriptions of historic liturgies must remain somewhat tentative.

At this point the lectionary begins to pick up on those fixed days commemorating persons and events beyond the life of Christ. May 1, for example, celebrates the prophet Jeremiah.

54. **They gather before Holy Golgotha on the day of the appearance of the Holy Cross in the sky (May 7):**

Psalm 97 (antiphon: v. 6: "The heavens proclaim his justice; all the peoples have seen his glory!")

Apostle: Galatians 6:14-18

Letter of Cyril, Bishop of Jerusalem, to the Emperor Constantius, on the subject of the appearance of the sign of the Holy Cross in the sky.

Alleluia: Psalm 96 (v. 1: "Bless the Lord with a new song.")

Gospel: Matthew 24:30-35

55. **Commemoration of the infants killed by King Herod (May 9), in Bethlehem:**

Psalm 8 (antiphon: v. 2: "Out of the mouths of infants, of babes at the breast, you have ordained praise.")

Apostle: Acts 12:1-24

Apostle: Hebrews 2:14-18

Alleluia: Psalm 103 (v. 1: "Bless the Lord, O my soul.")

Gospel: Matthew 2:16-18

56. **Commemoration of the Emperor Constantine (May 22), at the Holy Martyrium:**

Psalm 132 (antiphon: v. 1: "Lord, do not forget the trials of David.")

Apostle: 1 Timothy 2:1-7

Alleluia: Psalm 21 (v. 1: "Lord, in your power we rejoice.")

Gospel: Luke 7:1-10

57. **The Holy Ascension of Christ, forty days after Easter:**

Psalm 47 (antiphon: v. 5: "God is gone up in the midst of praise, and our Lord with the sound of the trumpet!")

Apostle: Acts 1:1-14

Alleluia: Psalm 24 (v. 1: "The earth is the Lord's and everything in it.")

Gospel: Luke 24:41-53

58. **Holy Pentecost, on Sunday, at the Holy Martyrium:**

Psalm 143 (antiphon: v. 10b: "May your good Spirit guide me through a smooth land.")

Apostle: Acts 2:1-21

Alleluia: Psalm 94 (v. 1: "O Lord, the God who avenges, O God who avenges, shine forth!")

Gospel: John 14:15-24

And immediately after the dismissal at the Martyrium, at the third hour, at Holy Sion:

This day commemorated a miraculous event in the life of the Jerusalem church in A.D. 351: the appearing of a cross in the sky over the city. Cyril's letter to the emperor stated that the whole city saw the cross, which extended from Golgotha to the Mount of Olives.

During this period, the evolution of the yearly calendar is heading toward an increasing number of feasts. The Gospel of Luke and the Acts of the Apostles are important in this evolution because they give dates for relating events to each other (e.g., Christ's ascension to heaven forty days after the Resurrection and the outpouring of the Spirit ten days later).

The roving quality of Jerusalem's worship can be seen on the day of Pentecost, the Sunday fifty days after Easter, which celebrates the outpouring of the Holy Spirit, according to Acts 2. Worship began in the Martyrium (Egeria noted that the earlier service in the Anastasis occurred every Sunday; see her diary above) and then moved to Sion, the traditional site for the Spirit's outpouring, at the hour at which it occurred.

Psalm 143 (antiphon: v. 10b: "May your good Spirit guide me through a smooth land.")

Apostle: Acts 2:1-21

Alleluia: Psalm 94 (v. 1: "O Lord, the God who avenges, O God who avenges, shine forth!")

Gospel: John 14:25-29

The same day of Sunday, at the tenth hour, on the Holy Mount of Olives, at the Summit:

Psalm 143 (antiphon: v. 10b: "May your good Spirit guide me through a smooth land.")

Apostle: Acts 2:1-21

Alleluia, Psalm 94 (v. 1: "O Lord, the God who avenges, O God who avenges, shine forth!")

Gospel: John 16:5-14

After the Gospel, they kneel, and this scripture [the Scriptures likely meant are those immediately preceding] is performed three times, as in all the holy places.

In the evening, they go to Holy Sion:

Psalm 143 (antiphon: v. 10b: "May your good Spirit guide me through a smooth land.")

Gospel: John 14:15-24

59. **Deposition of the Prophet Zechariah (June 10):**

Psalm 26 (antiphon: v. 8: "Lord, I have loved the beauty of your house, and the place of the habitation of your glory!")

Old Testament: Zechariah 3:7-4:9

Apostle: 1 Corinthians 12:26-13:10

Alleluia: Psalm 116:1-9 (v. 1: "I love the Lord because he heard my cry.")

Gospel: John 1:43-51

60. **Commemoration of the Prophet Elisha (June 14):**

Psalm 116 (antiphon: v. 15: "Precious in the sight of the Lord is the death of his saints.")

Old Testament: 2 Kings 13:14-21

Apostle: Hebrews 11:32-40

Alleluia: Psalm 116:1-9 (v. 1: "I love the Lord because he heard my cry.")

Gospel: Luke 4:25-41

61. **Commemoration of the Ark of the Covenant (July 2), at Kiriathiarim [Kiriathiarim is a site west of Jerusalem, also known as Kiriath-Jearim or Deir el-Azar]:**

Psalm 132 (antiphon: v. 8: "Rise up, Lord, from your rest, you and the ark of your holiness!")

Old Testament: 1 Samuel 6:19-7:2a

Old Testament: 2 Samuel 6:12b-19

Apostle: Hebrews 9:1-10

Alleluia: Psalm 98 (v. 1: "Sing to the Lord a new song.")

Gospel: Matthew 5:17-20

62. **Deposition of the Prophet Isaiah (July 6):**

Psalm 116 (antiphon: v. 15: "Precious in the sight of the Lord is the death of his saints.")

Old Testament: Isaiah 6:1-10

Apostle: Ephesians 4:7-16

Alleluia: Psalm 116:1-9 (v. 1: "I love the Lord because he heard my cry.")

Gospel: Luke 4:14-22a

63. **Commemoration of the Maccabees (August 1):**

Psalm 116 (antiphon: v. 15: "Precious in the sight of the Lord is the death of his saints.")

Apocrypha: 2 Maccabees 6:18-7:42

Apostle: Hebrews 11:32-12:13

Alleluia: Psalm 116:1-9 (v. 1: "I love the Lord because he heard my cry.")

Gospel: Matthew 5:17-20

> The Maccabees were the Jews who fought for and won independence from a Syrian yoke in the second century before Christ.

64. **Commemoration of Mary, the *Theotokos* (August 15), at the second mile from Bethlehem:**

Psalm 132 (antiphon: v. 8: "Arise, Lord, to your resting place, you and the ark of your holiness!")

Old Testament: Isaiah 7:10-16a

Apostle: Galatians 3:29-4:7

Alleluia: Psalm 110:1-7 (v. 1: "The Lord says to my Lord, 'Sit at my right hand.'")

Gospel: Luke 2:1-7

65. **Commemoration of the Apostle Thomas and of other saints (August 23), at Bethpage:**

Psalm 19 (antiphon: v. 4: "Their voice is gone out into all the earth, and their words to the ends of the world!")

Apostle: Acts 1:12-14

Apostle: 1 Corinthians 12:26-13:10

Alleluia: Psalm 27 (v. 1: "The Lord is my light and my salvation.")

Gospel: John 20:24-31

66. **Commemoration of John the Baptizer (August 29)**

Psalm 116 (antiphon: v. 15: "Precious in the sight of the Lord is the death of his saints.")

Apostle: Acts 13:16-42

> *Theotokos* means "God-bearer." To use this term for Mary was a way for the ancient church to affirm the divinity of Jesus Christ, i.e., the one Mary bore was not only a man but also God. The reason why these Scriptures were read is straightforward: they focus on the birth of Jesus Christ. The choice of Psalm 132, however, is more subtle because it relies on a figurative interpretation of the ark of the covenant in the Old Testament. Just as God's glory filled the Tabernacle and rested upon the ark, so the power of God filled Mary in the conception of Jesus.

Alleluia: Psalm 116:1-9 (v. 1: "I love the Lord, because he heard my cry.")

Gospel: Matthew 14:1-12

67. **Dedication of the Holy Places of Jerusalem (September 13), at the Holy Anastasis:**

Psalm 65 (antiphon: v. 1: "To you, God, belongs the praise in Sion, and to you is presented prayer in Jerusalem!")

Apostle: 1 Timothy 3:14-16

Alleluia: Psalm 147:12-20 (v. 12: "Extol the Lord, O Jerusalem! Praise your God, O Sion!")

Gospel: John 10:22-42

68. **On the second day, they gather in the Holy Martyrium, and the same scripture is performed.** [The Scriptures likely meant are those immediately preceding this.] **And on the same day, they display the Venerable Cross to all the assembly.**

69. **Commemoration of the Apostle Phillip (November 15):**

Psalm 19 (antiphon: v. 4: "Their voice is gone out into all the earth, their words to the ends of the world!")

Apostle: Acts 8:26-40

Alleluia: Psalm 47 (v. 1: "Clap your hands, all you nations!")

Gospel: John 1:43-51

70. **Commemoration of the Apostle Andrew (November 30):**

Psalm 19 (antiphon: v. 4: "Their voice is gone out into all the earth, their words to the ends of the world!")

Apostle: 1 Corinthians 12:26-14:4

Alleluia: Psalm 95 (v. 1: "Come, let us sing for joy to the Lord!")

Gospel: John 1:35-44

Note that in this early period Jerusalem had not established a Nativity celebration on December 25. Jerusalem's epiphany feast on January 6 had this emphasis. Other Eastern churches remembered the baptism of Christ on January 6, however.

71. **Commemoration of James and of David (December 25), at Holy Sion:**

During this day, in other cities, they celebrate the Nativity of Christ.

Psalm 132 (antiphon: v. 1: "Lord, do not forget the trials of David.")

Old Testament: 2 Samuel 5:1-10

Apostle: Acts 15:1-29

Alleluia: Psalm 110:1-7 (v. 1: "The Lord says to my Lord, 'Sit at my right hand.'")

Gospel: Matthew 22:41-46

72. **Commemoration of Saint Stephen (December 27):**

Psalm 5 (antiphon: v. 12: "Lord, as with a shield you have crowned us with your favor.")

Apostle: Acts 6:8-8:2

Alleluia: Psalm 21 (v. 1: "O Lord, the king rejoices in your strength.")

Gospel: John 12:24-26

73. Commemoration of Paul and of Peter, Apostles (December 28):

Psalm 19 (antiphon: v. 4: "Their voice is gone out into all the earth, their words to the
   ends of the world!")

Apostle: 2 Peter 1:12-19

Apostle: 2 Timothy 4:1-8

Alleluia: Psalm 47 (v. 1: "Clap your hands, all you nations.")

Gospel: John 21:15-19

74. Commemoration of the Apostle James and of John the Evangelist (December 29):

Psalm 96 (antiphon: v. 2b: "Proclaim salvation from day to day.")

Apostle: James 1:1-12

Apostle: 1 John 1:1-9

Alleluia: Psalm 85 (v. 1: "You showed favor to your land, O Lord.")

Gospel: John 21:20-25

Source: The lectionary describing Jerusalem Scripture practices is best attested in Armenian sources. The chief among these is Codex Armenian Jerusalem 121, a manuscript from the fifth century. Athanase Renoux has published the critical edition of this manuscript in Armenian with a French translation, introduction, and commentary as "Le Codex Arménien Jérusalem 121," *Patrologia Orientalis* 36/2 (1971), pp.210-373. This manuscript has fewer gaps than the manuscript Paris B.N. arm. 44, which was the basis of F. C. Conybeare's *Rituale Armenorum* (1896). The English translation is new for this publication.

The Communion Prayer Likely Used in Jerusalem

*This prayer, called an **anaphora**, is known as that of St. James, the brother of the Lord, although that linkage is highly unlikely. What is more likely is that this prayer was said in Jerusalem at the end of the fourth century or the beginning of the fifth as the consecratory prayer in Communion. It has long been regarded as one of the most important windows into fourth-century Eucharistic practices in the East and a key connection between the various Communion prayers developing at the time. Was it the prayer that Cyril would have used as bishop? It is impossible to know with absolute certainty because his homiletical allusions to the prayer do not allow a full reconstruction of what he used.*

This kind of prayer is called an anaphora because, roughly translated, the word means to lift or send up prayer. The opening lines, which may refer to Paul's command in Colossians 3:2 ("Set your hearts on things above..."), call for the congregation to do exactly that.

The bishop* begins:

May the love of our God and Father, the grace of our Lord, God, and Savior Jesus Christ, and the fellowship and the gifts of the Holy Spirit be with you all.

The people respond:

And with your spirit.

Next the bishop says:

Let us lift up our mind and our hearts.

And the people respond:

We lift them up to the Lord.

Then the bishop says:

Let us give thanks to the Lord.

And the people respond:

It is fitting and right.

This instruction for the bishop to pray privately (i.e., in a hushed or whispered voice) shows part of the evolution of liturgical practice. Whereas the earliest centuries of the church indicate that prayers were said audibly in church, by the late patristic period some prayers, including the Eucharistic anaphora, were said so that people could not hear them. This tendency will increase in upcoming centuries.

The bishop, bowing, prays privately:

How truly it is fitting and right, proper and obligatory, to praise you, to celebrate you in song, to bless you, to adore you, to glorify you, to give you thanks, the creator of all creation, visible and invisible, the storehouse of eternal treasures, the spring of life and immortality, the God and Master of all.

*The Greek word used here and consistently through this prayer, *hiereus*, means "priest."

The heavens—even the heavens of heavens—and all their powers, the sun, moon, and the entire choir of stars, earth, sea, and all that is in them sing your praises. The heavenly Jerusalem, the assembly of the elect, the church of the first-born enrolled in heaven, the spirits of righteous people and prophets, the souls of martyrs and apostles sing your praise. Angels, archangels, thrones, dominions, principalities, and powers—even powers who ought to be fearful—sing your praises. The multi-eyed cherubim and six-winged seraphim (two wings covering their own faces, two their feet, and two flying) shout to one another with untiring mouths and never-silent hymns to God.

The bishop again prays aloud:

With clear voice they proclaim the triumphal hymn of your magnificent glory, exulting, praising, crying, and saying:

The people say:

Holy, holy, holy, Lord of Hosts; heaven and earth are full of your glory. Hosanna in the highest. Blessed is he who has come and is coming in the name of the Lord. Hosanna in the highest.

And the bishop, standing up and making the sign of the cross over the Communion elements, says to himself:

You are holy, King of the ages, Lord and Giver of all holiness. And holy is your only-begotten Son, our Lord Jesus Christ, through whom you made all things. And holy too is your Spirit, holy in every way, who searches out all things, even your depths, you who are [our] God and Father.

He bows and says:

You are holy, almighty, omnipotent, fully able, fearful, good, and compassionate. You have abundant sympathy for your handiwork. You made a human from the earth in your image and likeness. You gave him the delight of paradise. When the human transgressed your commandment and fell, you neither despised nor abandoned him, for you are good. Instead, you disciplined him as a kindly father, you called him through the law, and you instructed him through the prophets.

Later you sent your only-begotten Son, our Lord Jesus Christ, into the world to renew and resuscitate your image by his coming. He came from heaven and was made flesh by the Holy Spirit and Mary, the Holy ever-Virgin and Mother of God. He dwelt among us and distributed everything for the salvation of our race.

He was willing to endure a voluntary and life-giving death on the cross, the sinless for us sinners. On the night when he was betrayed, or rather handed himself over, for the life and salvation of the world,

---

Rather than being focused on us, this Eucharistic prayer develops a strong cosmic note. As was common in classic ways of Christian praying, this prayer's naming and remembering practices are outwardly focused.

There are Trinitarian and narrative qualities to the prayer. The prayer is addressed to God the Father, who is the main actor, especially in what he has accomplished through Jesus Christ, the Son of God. Later in the prayer there will be a pleading for the Father to send the Holy Spirit.

At this point the bishop stands up, takes the bread, makes the sign of the cross, and says:
he took bread in his holy, undefiled, blameless, and immortal hands. He looked up to heaven and showed it to you, God and Father. He gave thanks, blessed, sanctified, and broke it, and he gave it to his holy and blessed disciples and apostles, saying,

Now the bishop puts the bread down and says aloud:
Take, eat. This is my body, broken for you and shared for the forgiveness of sins.

The people respond:
Amen.

Then the bishop takes the cup, makes the sign of the cross, and says privately:
Likewise, after supper he took the cup and mixed wine and water in it. He looked up to heaven and showed it to you, his God and Father. He gave thanks, blessed, and sanctified it, filling it by the Holy Spirit. Then he shared it with his holy and blessed disciples and apostles, saying,

Communion was not only received; it was also offered. The church was not merely a passive recipient in the Eucharist. Rather, participating in, or offering, the sacrament was the supreme act of adoration and thanksgiving. Remember how Egeria usually calls it the "oblation" or "offering."

Then he puts the cup down and says aloud:
Drink from it, all of you. This is my blood of the new covenant, which, for you and for many, is poured out and shared for the forgiveness of sins.

The people respond:
Amen.

Then the bishop stands and says privately:
Do this for my remembrance. For as often as you eat this bread and drink this cup, you proclaim the death of the Son of Man and confess his resurrection, until he comes.

The present deacons respond:
We believe and confess.

And the people respond:
Your death, Lord, we proclaim, and your resurrection we confess.

One of the ways to make worship scriptural is to fill it with the words of Scripture. Consider how the anaphora at this point uses Colossians 2:14, 1 Corinthians 2:9, and Isaiah 64:4 to pray.

Then the bishop makes the sign of the cross, bows, and says privately:
We, sinners, therefore, remember his life-giving sufferings, his saving cross, his death, his burial, and his resurrection from the dead on the third day. We remember his ascension to heaven, his sitting down at your right hand, you who are our God and Father, and his glorious and fearful second-coming. He will come with glory to judge the living and the dead and will

reward us according to our works.—Spare us, Lord our God [repeated three times].—According to your compassion, we offer you, Master, this awesome and bloodless sacrifice. We ask that you neither deal with us according to our sins nor repay us according to our iniquities. According to your gentleness and unspeakable loving-kindness for us, pass over and blot out the handwriting that is against us, the ones pleading to you. Grant us your heavenly and eternal gifts, which no eye has seen, nor ear heard, nor the human heart conceived what you, O God, have prepared for those who love you.

Next the bishop repeats three times:
And do not dismiss your people on account of me and my sins, O Lord, lover of humanity.

Then the bishop prays aloud:
For your people and your Church plead with you.

And the people respond:
Have mercy on us, Lord God, the Father Almighty.

Now the bishop stands up and says privately:
Have mercy on us, Lord God, the Father Almighty. Have mercy on us, God, our Savior. Have mercy on us, O God, according to your great mercy. Pour out your all-Holy Spirit upon us and upon these holy gifts set before you.

The bishop bows and continues:
The Lord and maker of life, who shares the throne and the kingdom with you, God the Father and your only-begotten Son, co-ruler, consubstantial and co-eternal. Pour forth your Holy Spirit, who spoke in the law and the prophets and in your new covenant, who descended in the likeness of a dove upon our Lord Jesus Christ in the River Jordan and remained upon him, who descended upon your holy apostles in the likeness of fiery tongues in the Upper Room of the holy and glorious Zion on the day of the holy Pentecost.

Compare this section with the Nicene Creed. The controversies that led to the creed are still fresh in the life of the church. These words clearly contain explicit doctrinal statements embedded in the very language of the prayers.

Still standing, the bishop continues, privately:
Send down, Master, your all-Holy Spirit on us and on the holy gifts placed here.

[Then he says aloud]:
Sanctify them by his holy, good, and glorious coming, and make this bread the holy body of Christ.

The people respond:
Amen.

Next the bishop says:

And this cup, the priceless blood of Christ.

And the people respond:

Amen.

Now the bishop stands up and says privately:

That these gifts may become to all who share in them the forgiveness of sins, eternal life, and sanctification of souls and bodies. May they bring forth good works to strengthen your holy, catholic, and apostolic Church, which you founded on the rock of faith, so that the gates of hell would not prevail against it. May they rescue your Church from every heresy, from the scandals of those who work lawlessness, and from the enemies who have risen and still do rise up until the consummation of the age.

The clerics alone answer:

Amen.

Then the bishop makes the sign of the cross and bows:

We offer to you, Master, for your holy places also, which you made glorious by the appearing of your Christ and the arrival of your all-Holy Spirit. We offer to you principally for holy and glorious Zion, the mother of all the churches, and for your holy, catholic, and apostolic Church which exists throughout the world. Even now, Master, lavish it with the gifts of your Holy Spirit.

If a parish priest, not a bishop, was using this prayer, he would have prayed for the bishop ("Father N.") at this point.

Remember, Lord, also our holy fathers and bishops in the Church, who preach correctly your word of truth throughout the world. We pray for our holy Father N., and all his clergy and priesthood. Grant to him a long life. Preserve him for a long time to shepherd your flock in all piety and dignity.

Remember, Lord, the honorable presbytery here and everywhere, the diaconate in Christ, all the other ministers, every ecclesiastical order and fraternity we have in Christ, and all Christ-loving people.

As was typical for the time, the church's intercessory prayers were as broad as the Lordship of Jesus Christ. Notice the wide expanse of requests in this next section, from creation to family members to public officials.

Remember, Lord, the priests who stand with us in this holy hour, before your holy altar, for the offering of the holy and bloodless sacrifice. Give to them and us your word to open our mouths to the glory and praise of your all-holy name.

Remember, Lord, according to the multitude of your mercy and your pity, me also, your humble, sinful, and unworthy servant. Visit me with pity and compassion, and free and snatch me from those who persecute me, O Lord, the Lord of hosts. Since sin abounds in me, let your grace much more abound.

Remember, Lord, also the deacons who gather around your holy altar, and grant them a blameless life. Preserve their ministry unspotted and guide their walk through life.

Remember, Lord, our God, your holy and royal city and all of the city and region, and grant those who live therein sound faith and reverence. Give them peace and security.

Remember, Lord, our most pious and Christ-loving emperor, his pious and Christ-loving empress, all his court and his army. Help them and give them victory. Take up arms and shield; rise up to help him. Subject to our emperor all the warlike and barbarous nations that desire war. Train his counsel, that we may lead a quiet and peaceful life in all piety and reverence.

Remember, Lord, the Christians who come to worship at the holy sites of Christ.

Remember, Lord, Christians at sea, on the road, and traveling, our fathers and brothers in chains and prisons, in captivity and exile, in mines and tortures and bitter slavery. Give to each of them a peaceful return home.

Remember, Lord, those growing old and feeble, those who languish, suffer, or are infested by unclean spirits. We pray for their speedy healing and salvation by you, O God.

Remember, Lord, every Christian soul vexed and afflicted, in need of your mercy and help, O God. Recover the wandering and indigent.

Remember, Lord, our venerable fathers and brothers who live in virginity, piety, and self-discipline, and those who strive among mountains, dens, and caves of the earth. Remember the orthodox communities in every location and those who form a community in Christ here.

Remember, Lord, our fathers and brothers who labor and serve for your holy name.

Remember, Lord, all people for good. On all have mercy, Master. Reconcile us all; bring peace to the multitudes of your people. Demolish scandals, abolish wars, and bring to an end the divisions of the churches. Dissolve quickly the uprisings of the heresies, cast down the ferocity of the heathen, exalt the horn of the Christians, and give us your peace and your love, O God our Savior, the hope of all the ends of the earth.

Remember, Lord, temperate weather, peaceful showers, sufficient moisture, abundance of fruit, a good and perfect harvest, and the crown of the year of your goodness, for the eyes of all wait for you, and you give them their food in due season. You open your hand, satisfying the desire of every living thing.

Here the bishop nods toward the arch-deacon:
Remember, Lord, those who have brought and bring forth fruit in your holy churches, O God. Remember those who remember the poor and those who have asked us to remember them in our prayers.

Consider it worthy, Lord, to remember those who have offered the offerings today on your holy altar, and on behalf of those whom each one offered or had in mind, and those who are recounted to you.

Following a common biblical usage (e.g., Psalm 89:24), "horn" here refers to strength or power.

And the bishop mentions those whom he wishes who are in this present life:
Remember, Lord, also our parents, friends, relatives, and siblings.

Remember all these, Lord, whom we have remembered and those orthodox Christians we have not remembered. In turn give them heavenly for earthly goods, imperishable for perishable, eternal for temporary, according to the promise of your Christ, since you have power over life and death.

Consider it worthy to remember, also, Lord, those who have been well-pleasing to you from the beginning, through each generation: the holy fathers, patriarchs, prophets, apostles, martyrs, confessors, venerable teachers, and every righteous spirit perfected in the faith of your Christ.

Now the bishop repeats three times:
Hail, "highly favored one," the Lord is with you. Blessed are you among women, and blessed is the fruit of your womb, for you bore the Savior of our souls.

This snippet of praise to Mary, the mother of Jesus, is surely an addition to the text from after the fourth century. (Compare Luke 1:28.) It is helpful to remember that ancient liturgical texts are a little like onions: They have multiple layers of accumulated changes. Later manuscripts, as in this case, show the many-layered version, not the simpler version which is often the quest of the worship historian.

Next the bishop says aloud:
Especially remember our Holy, Blessed, and spotless Lady, Mary, the Mother of God, the ever-Virgin.

Then the deacon reads from the diptych of the living [an official list for commemorations]:
For salvation, peace, mercy, long life, and protection of our most holy patriarch, N., and the other venerable archbishops and bishops, the ones rightly speaking the word of truth in all the world of every ecclesiastical order.

For kings and all those in authority and power that we might lead a quiet and tranquil life in all piety and dignity.

Also for the presbyters, deacons, deaconesses, sub-deacons, readers, exorcists, interpreters, cantors, monks, virgins, widows, orphans, the chaste, and those living in holy marriage and for lovers of Christ.

And the bishop calls out and says:
Especially for the all-holy and blessed, our immaculate Lady, the mother of God and ever-Virgin, Mary.

And the clergy alone answer privately:
Remember, Lord, our God.

Now the bishop bows down and says:
Holy John, the prophet, forerunner and Baptist.

The Holy Apostles Peter, Paul, Andrew, James, John, Philip, Bartholomew, Thomas, Matthew, James, Simon, Jude, Matthias;

Mark and Luke, the evangelists.

The holy prophets and patriarchs and the just.

Holy Stephen, the first deacon and first martyr.

The holy martyrs and confessors, who for Christ our true God witnessed and made the good confession.

The infants who were put to death by King Herod.

The holy martyrs Procopius, Theodore, Cyrus, John, George, Leontius, Sergius, Bacchus, Cosmas, Damian, Sabinianus, Paul, Babilas, Agathangelus, Eustratius and those who fought along with him.

The holy forty, the holy forty-five.

Holy Thecla, the first woman martyr.

The holy women who brought the myrrh.

The holy women martyrs Tatte, Febronia, Anastasia, Euphemia, Sophia, Barbara, Juliana, Irene, Faith, Hope, and Grace.

In the tumultuous times in the late patristic period and following, including and excluding names in these lists are ways of making statements about doctrine, church fellowship, and politics, all of which are intertwined.

Remember, Lord God, our holy fathers and archbishops who, from holy James, the apostle and brother of the Lord and first archbishop, down to Leo and Athanasius, have guarded the orthodoxy of the archbishops of the holy city of Christ our Lord.

And remember those who have been archbishops from the beginning, from our holy and blessed Father Eneas, an apostolic man and first of the bishops, down to Sophronius and John.

This section, with its naming of ecumenical councils, obviously comes from a period after the fourth century, since it names meetings occurring afterwards.

Remember, Lord, our holy Fathers and teachers: Clement, Timothy, Ignatius, Dionysius, Irenaeus, Gregory, Alexander, Eustathius, Athanasius, Basil, Gregory, Gregory, Ambrose, Amphilochius, Liberius, Damasus, John, Epiphanius, Theophilus, Celestinus, Augustine, Cyril, Leo, Proclus, Proterius, Felix, Hormisdas, Eulogius, Ephraem, Anastasius, Theodore, Martin, Agathon, and Sophronius.

Prayers for the dead are a common feature of early Christian spirituality, attested in ancient liturgies as well as catacomb inscriptions and perhaps influenced by Apocryphal Jewish texts which did not make the biblical canon. To be included in a church's list of the deceased was a sign of one's orthodoxy in the eyes of the church.

Remember, Lord, the six holy, great, and ecumenical councils: the three hundred and eighteen of Nicea, the one hundred and fifty of Constantinople, the two hundred of the first Ephesus, the six hundred and thirty of Chalcedon, the one hundred and sixty-four of the fifth holy council, the two hundred and eighty-nine of the sixth holy council, and the other holy councils and bishops who in all the world handle the word of truth rightly with sound faith.

Remember, Lord, our holy Fathers and ascetics: Paul, Antony, Charito, Paul, Pachomius, Hamoun, Theodore, Hilarion, Arsenius, Macarius, Sisoïus, John, Pambo, Poemen, Nilus,

Isidore, Ephrem, Symeon, Symeon, Theodosius, Saba, Saba, Euthymius, Theoctistus, Gerasimus, Pantaleon, Maximus, Anastasius, Cosmas, and John.

Remember, Lord, our holy fathers who were put to death by the barbarians in the holy mountain of Sinai and in Raitho, our other venerable fathers and orthodox ascetics, and all the saints. Not because we are worthy to keep the memory of their blessedness, but in order that they, standing by your awe-ful and fearful seat of judgment, may keep the memory of our trouble.

Remember, Lord, presbyters, deacons, deaconesses, subdeacons, readers, exorcists, interpreters, cantors, monks, virgins, widows, orphans, the chaste, and all those perfected by faith in the community of your holy, catholic, and apostolic Church.

Remember, Lord, the pious and faithful emperors Constantine, Helena, Theodosius the Great, Marcianus, Pulcheria, Leo, Justinian, Constantine, those who reigned after them in piety and faith, and all Christ-loving orthodox laity who now sleep in death in the faith and sign of Christ.

And for the peace and stability of all the saints of the churches of God and for the sake of whomever offers and is remembering and for the people who love Christ assembled here, both men and women.

And then the bishop says privately:
Remember Holy John the prophet, forerunner and the Baptist. Remember the saints generally and the praiseworthy apostles and saint N., whose memory we keep. Remember all your saints whose supplications visit us, O God, and remember, O Lord, all those who sleep in the hope of the Resurrection of eternal life and make it so that they may rest when they look upon the light of your face.

Remember, Lord, our parents and friends and relatives.

And after them he makes mention of those orthodox whom he wishes:
Remember all orthodox Christians, Lord, the God of the spirits and of all flesh, those whom we have remembered and whom we have not. Give them rest in the land of the living, in your kingdom, in the delight of paradise, in the bosom of Abraham, Isaac, and Jacob, our holy fathers, from where anguish, gloom, and sighing have flown, where the light of your countenance looks on them and enlightens them forever. Guide in peace the ends of our lives to be worthily Christian, pleasing to you, and sinless, Lord. Gather us under the feet of your elect, whenever

you will and as you will, only without shame and transgressions, through your only-begotten Son, our Lord and God and Savior Jesus Christ, for he alone has appeared on earth without sin.

The bishop concludes out loud:
Remember first of all, Lord, our most holy father and patriarch, N., of our holy city of Christ our God, and those who with him [i.e., the patriarch] are four of the holy, great, ecumenical, orthodox patriarchs, namely, Benedict of Rome, Nicholas of Constantinople, Agapius of Antioch, and Elias of the Great City of Alexandria, and N., our archbishop, to all these grant salvation for your holy churches in peace.

Now the deacon prays:
We pray for the peace and stability of the whole world and the holy churches of God. We pray for all those for whom each of us have offered prayers or kept in mind and for all the people gathered here, both men and women.

And the bishop says:
Through whom, as a good God and a people-loving Master, to us and them,

The people continue:
remit, forgive, pardon, O God, our sins, voluntary and involuntary, known and unknown,

And the bishop concludes alone:
By the grace, compassion, and love of your Christ, with whom you are blessed and glorified, with your all-Holy and life-giving Spirit, now and always and to the ages of ages. Amen.

> PRAYER AND LORD'S PRAYER
> PRAYER OF INCLINATION
> PRAYER OF ELEVATION AND FRACTION

Now the bishop raises the gift and says aloud:
The holy things for the holy people.

The people respond:
One is holy. One is Lord, Jesus Christ, to the glory of God the Father, with the Holy Spirit. To him be glory to the ages of ages.

> COMMUNION
> INCENSE-PRAYERS

It was common for multiple prayers to accumulate in ancient liturgies. Eventually the liturgy of St. James after the anaphora (i.e., the consecratory prayer) included multiple prayers, including the prayer of inclination (asking for God's blessing while worshipers bowed), the prayer of elevation and fraction (worshiping God and asking for his power while holding up the Communion elements and dividing the bread), and incense-prayers (praising God by sending up incense).

PRAYER OF INCLINATION

THANKSGIVING FOR COMMUNION

DISMISSAL

PRAYER (in sacristy)

Source: The Anaphora of St. James is translated from the standard critical edition in Greek (and Latin) by B. C. Mercier, *La Liturgie de S. Jacques Patrologia Orientalis* 26, 2 (Paris: Firmin-Didot, 1946). (This translation attempts to be faithful to the original and accessible for current readers. It is possible that sentences were shortened or lengthened without significant change to content for clarity and accessibility. Scholarly work should refer back to the original languages.) The key manuscript for the Greek version is ms. Vaticanus Graecus 2282 from the ninth century. An old English translation of the entire liturgy is found in F. E. Brightman's *Liturgies, Eastern and Western* (1896), based on a fourteenth-century manuscript. Another newer English translation of the anaphora can be found in Ronald Claud Dudley Jasper and G.J. Cuming, *Prayers of the Eucharist: Early and Reformed* (Collegeville, Minn.: Liturgical Press, 1990), pp. 88-99, based on ms. Vaticanus Graecus 2282. The standard critical edition in Syriac (with Latin translation) is O. Heiming, *Anaphorae Syriacae* (Rome, 1953).

The Liturgy of St. James, Historically Associated with Jerusalem

This ancient liturgy has many points of contact with the worship described by Cyril in his post-baptismal instructions (see "Sermons"). Historically attributed to James (the Lord's brother) and to Jerusalem, the current form reflects several additions made after the fourth century. Syriac, Armenian, and Georgian-speaking churches used it quite frequently. Manuscripts of the liturgy are inevitably from a later period and probably show development during the intervening centuries and therefore differences from what is found in more contemporaneous accounts of fourth-century worship. The Anaphora of James (see the preceding prayer) should be seen as situated in this sort of broader liturgy, although the two have been separated in this volume because the textual and translation traditions for the anaphora are somewhat different than those for the whole liturgy. Those differences allow one to approach the anaphora with a greater degree of confidence in its reflecting the late fourth century or early fifth century than the whole Liturgy of St. James.

The priest* begins:

O Sovereign Lord our God, do not condemn me, defiled with a multitude of sins. I come to this, your divine and heavenly mystery, not as worthy, but looking only to your goodness. I direct my voice to you: God, be merciful to me, a sinner. I have sinned against Heaven and before you. I am unworthy to come into the presence of this your holy and spiritual table, upon which your only-begotten Son, our Lord Jesus Christ, is mystically set forth as a sacrifice for me, a sinner, and stained with every spot. I present to you this supplication and thanksgiving that your Spirit the Comforter may be sent down upon me, strengthening and fitting me for this service. Count me worthy to make known without condemnation the word, delivered from you by me to the people, in Christ Jesus, our Lord, with whom you are blessed, together with your all-holy, good, life-giving, and consubstantial Spirit, now and ever, and to all eternity. Amen.

Notice the Trinitarian nature of the prayer: addressed to God the Father, who is remembered for his actions through the Son and petitioned for the Spirit. God has acted through the Son by the Spirit for us. Christians pray to the Father through the Son by the Spirit. The "logic" of the Trinitarian shape of salvation history is thus reflected in the classic Christian prayer's shape and content.

Standing beside the altar, the priest prays:

Glory to the Father, and to the Son, and to the Holy Spirit, the Triune light of the Godhead, which is unity subsisting in Trinity, divided, yet indivisible. The Trinity is the one God Almighty, whose glory the heavens declare, the earth his dominion, and the sea his might. Every living creature at all times proclaims his majesty. All glory, honor, and might, greatness and magnificence, are his, now and ever, and to all eternity. Amen.

---

* The Greek word *hierus* translated here as "priest," was translated as "bishop" in the previous section. Although the word *priest* is used in this section, following our source, these items would have been led by a bishop if present.

Sovereign Lord Jesus Christ, O Word of God, you freely offered yourself a blameless sacrifice upon the cross to God the Father. With the coal of double nature that touched the lips of the prophet with the tongs and took away his sins, touch also the hearts of us sinners, purify us from every stain, and present us holy beside your holy altar, that we may offer you a sacrifice of praise. Accept from us, your unprofitable servants, this incense as an odor of a sweet smell. Make fragrant the evil odor of our soul and body, and purify us with the sanctifying power of your all-holy Spirit. You alone are holy, who sanctifies and are communicated to the faithful. Glory is yours, with your eternal Father, and your all-holy, good, and life-giving Spirit, now and ever, to all eternity. Amen.

O beneficent King eternal, and Creator of the universe, receive your Church, coming to you through your Christ. Give to each what is profitable. Lead all to perfection, and make us perfectly worthy of the grace of your sanctification. Gather us together within your holy Church, which you have purchased by the precious blood of your only-begotten Son, and our Lord and Savior Jesus Christ, with whom you are blessed and glorified, together with your all-holy, good, and life-giving Spirit, now and ever, and to all eternity. Amen.

The deacon says:
Let us again pray to the Lord.

The priest prays as the service begins:
God, who accepted the gifts of Abel, the sacrifice of Noah and of Abram, the incense of Aaron and Zacharias, accept also from the hand of us sinners this incense as a sweet smell, and for remission of our sins and those of all your people. You are blessed, and glory is yours, Father, Son, and Holy Spirit, now and ever.

Then the deacon says to the priest:
Sir, pronounce the blessing.

The priest prays:
Our Lord and God, Jesus Christ, who through exceeding and unrestrained goodness and love was crucified and did not refuse to be pierced by the spear and nails, who provided this mysterious service as an everlasting memorial for us perpetually, bless your ministry, bless our entrance, and fully complete the presentation of this our service by your unutterable compassion, now and ever, and to all eternity. Amen.

The deacon says:
The Lord bless us, and make us worthy as angels to offer gifts and to sing the hymn of the divine **Trisagion** by the fullness and exceeding abundance of all the perfection of holiness, now and ever.

Presumably the prayers up to this point were prayers to prepare for worship.

Throughout the liturgy, Christ is explicitly mentioned as acting during worship to intercede between God the Father and the worshipers.

Trisagion means "thrice holy" and refers to the "Holy, Holy, Holy" of Isaiah's vision (Isa. 6:3).

Then the deacon begins to sing at the opening procession:

You, the only-begotten Son and Word of God, immortal, submitted for our salvation to become flesh of the holy God-mother, and ever-virgin Mary. You immutably became man and was crucified, O Christ our God. By your death, you tread death underfoot. As one of the Holy Trinity, glorified together with the Father and the Holy Spirit, save us.

This hymn, known as the Ho Monogenes ("The Only-Begotten"), is evidence that parts of the Liturgy of James come from after the time of Cyril. This particular piece normally is ascribed to the sixth century, nearly 200 years after Cyril.

The priest says this prayer from the gates to the altar:

God Almighty, Lord great in glory, who has given us an entrance into the Holy of holies, through the sojourning among humanity of your only-begotten Son, our Lord, and God, and Savior Jesus Christ, we supplicate and invoke your goodness, since we are fearful and trembling when about to stand at your holy altar. Send forth upon us, O God, your good grace, and sanctify our souls, bodies, and spirits. Turn our thoughts to piety in order that with a pure conscience we may bring to you gifts, offerings, and fruits for the remission of our transgressions and for the propitiation of all your people by the grace and mercies and loving-kindness of your only-begotten Son, with whom you are blessed to all eternity. Amen.

After the approach to the altar, the priest says:

Peace be to all.

The people respond:

And to your spirit.

The priest says:

The Lord bless us all, and sanctify us for the entrance and celebration of the divine and pure mysteries, giving rest to the blessed souls among the good and just, by his grace and loving-kindness, now and ever, and to all eternity. Amen.

Next the deacon says the bidding prayer:

In peace, let us pray to the Lord.

For the peace that is from above, for God's love to humanity, and for the salvation of our souls, let us pray to the Lord.

For the peace of the whole world, for the unity of all the holy churches of God, let us pray to the Lord.

For the remission of our sins and the forgiveness of our transgressions, and for our deliverance from all tribulation, wrath, danger, and distress and from the uprising of our enemies, let us pray to the Lord.

The "singers" were probably a choir, which began to appear in descriptions of worship in the fourth century and which became increasingly apparent in subsequent centuries.

Then the singers sing the Trisagion Hymn:

Holy God, holy mighty, holy immortal, have mercy upon us.

The instruction for the priest to pray "aloud" indicates a practice that grew in late antiquity, namely, a growing number of prayers said by presiders in hushed tones. Although it added to a sense of mystery in worship, it also meant that worshipers could not hear the theological content of the prayers, and possibly that things other than the main liturgical actions drew their attention during a service. Of course, even if a prayer was said out loud, the fact that the priest often prayed while bowing (not the easiest position from which to project one's voice) would have meant that few would have heard anyway. There were no microphones to help.

This liturgy, like other patristic liturgies, follows a common order: introductory rites and entrance, a substantial time of Bible reading and proclamation, then acts of tabling (the main intercessions, the offering, the exchange of the kiss of peace, the Great Thanksgiving prayed during Communion, and reception), and a final dismissal. Compare this to your experience of a typical worship service. When do you first hear Scripture read? How much Scripture is read? Do our services have the same range of worship activity and prayer?

Afterward, the priest prays privately, bowing:

O compassionate and merciful, long-suffering, and very gracious and true God, look from your prepared dwelling-place, hear us, and deliver us from every temptation of the devil and of humanity. Do not withhold your aid from us, nor pile on us chastisements too heavy for our strength, for we are unable to overcome what is opposed to us. But you are able, Lord, to save us from everything that is against us. Save us, O God, from the difficulties of this world, according to your goodness, in order that, having drawn nigh with a pure conscience to your holy altar, we may send up to you without condemnation the blessed hymn Trisagion, together with the heavenly powers, and that, having performed the service, well pleasing to you, we may be counted worthy of eternal life.

Then the priest prays aloud:

Because you are holy, Lord our God, and dwell and abide in holy places, we send up the praise and the hymn Trisagion to you, the Father, the Son, and the Holy Spirit, now and ever, and to all eternity.

The people respond:

Amen.

The priest says:

Peace be to all.

The people respond:

And to your spirit.

The singers respond:

Alleluia.

Then there are read in order the holy oracles of the Old Testament, and of the prophets. The incarnation of the Son of God is set forth, his sufferings and resurrection from the dead, his ascension into heaven, and his second appearing with glory. This takes place daily in the holy and divine service.

After the reading and instruction, the deacon says:

Let us all say, Lord, be merciful.

    Lord Almighty, the God of our fathers,

    We pray to you, hear us.

For the peace which is from above, and for the salvation of our souls,

Let us pray to the Lord.

For the peace of the whole world, and the unity of all the holy churches of God,

Let us pray to the Lord.

For the salvation and help of all the Christ-loving people,

We pray to you, Lord, hear us.

For our deliverance from all tribulation, wrath, danger, distress, captivity, bitter death, and our iniquities,

We pray to you, hear us.

For the people standing round, and waiting for the rich and plenteous mercy that is from you,

We pray to you, be merciful and gracious.

Save your people, O Lord, and bless your inheritance.

Visit your world in mercy and compassion.

Exalt the horn of Christians by the power of the precious and life-giving cross.

We ask you, most merciful Lord, hear us praying to you, and have mercy upon us.

The people repeat three times:

Lord, have mercy on us.

Then the deacon invites the people to pray:

For the remission of our sins and the forgiveness of our transgressions, and for our deliverance from all tribulation, wrath, danger, and distress, let us pray to the Lord.

Let us all pray to the Lord, that we may pass the whole day, perfect, holy, peaceful, and without sin.

Let us ask from the Lord a messenger of peace, a faithful guide, a guardian of our souls and bodies.

Let us pray to the Lord for forgiveness and remission of our sins and transgressions.

Let us ask from the Lord the things which are good and proper for our souls, and peace for the world.

Let us pray to the Lord, that we may spend the remaining period of our lives in peace and health.

Let us pray that the close of our lives may be Christian, without pain and without shame, and a good plea at the dread and awful judgment-seat of Christ.

This liturgy is chock-full of prayers of various types and lengths. It is a regular feature of ancient worship to pray. Prayers are the essence of worship. Other than songs, how many prayers (and what different kinds of prayer) does your church's worship have?

Based on comparable prayers elsewhere, it is likely that the choir (singers) or people sang short responses back to the deacon's invitations to pray, which themselves might have been sung. Protestant assumptions about clearly distinguishing between musical and non-musical parts of a service should not apply.

The priest says:

For you are the gospel and the light, Savior and keeper of our souls and bodies, God, and your only-begotten Son, and your all-holy Spirit, now and ever.

The people respond:

Amen.

The priest prays privately:

God, who has taught us your divine and saving oracles, enlighten the souls of us sinners for the comprehension of the things which have been before spoken, so that we may not only be seen to be hearers of spiritual things, but also doers of good deeds, striving after guileless faith, blameless life, and pure conversation.

The priest says aloud:

In Christ Jesus our Lord, with whom you are blessed, together with your all-holy, good, and life-giving Spirit, now and always, and forever.

The people respond:

Amen.

Then the priest says:

Peace be to all.

And the people respond:

And to your spirit.

The deacon instructs:

Let us bow our heads to the Lord.

The people respond:

To you, Lord.

The priest prays privately:

O sovereign giver of life and provider of good things, who gave to mankind the blessed hope of eternal life, our Lord Jesus Christ, count us worthy in holiness, and perfect this, your divine service, to the enjoyment of future blessedness.

The priest says aloud:

So that, guarded by your power at all times, and led into the light of truth, we may send up the praise and the thanksgiving to you, the Father, the Son, and the Holy Spirit, now and ever.

The people respond:

Amen.

The deacon instructs:

Let none of the catechumens, none of the unbaptized, none of those who are unable to join with us in prayer, remain. Look at one another. Guard the door. Everyone stand: Let us again pray to the Lord.

As is typical in ancient liturgies, the deacon makes sure that only the baptized remain for the latter half of the worship service.

Then the priest says the prayer of incense:

Sovereign Almighty, King of Glory, who knew all things before their creation, show yourself to us, who call on you at this holy hour. Redeem us from the shame of our transgressions. Cleanse our minds and our thoughts from impure desires, from worldly deceit, from all influence of the devil. Accept from the hands of us sinners this incense, as you accepted the offering of Abel, Noah, Aaron, Samuel, and of all your saints. Guard us from everything evil, and preserve us for continually pleasing, worshiping, and glorifying you, the Father, and your only-begotten Son, and your all-holy Spirit, now and always, and for ever.

And the readers begin the Cherubic Hymn:

Let all mortal flesh be silent, stand with fear and trembling, and meditate on nothing earthly within itself: For the King of kings and Lord of lords, Christ our God, comes forward to be sacrificed, and to be given for food to the faithful. The bands of angels go before him with every power and dominion, the many-eyed cherubim, and the six-winged seraphim, covering their faces, and crying aloud the hymn, "Alleluia, Alleluia, Alleluia."

Does this remind you of a hymn you know? As noted in the introduction, this liturgy inspired the hymn "Let All Mortal Flesh Keep Silence."

The priest brings in the holy gifts and says:

O God, our God, who sent forth the heavenly bread, the food of the whole world, our Lord Jesus Christ, to be a Savior, Redeemer, and Benefactor, blessing and sanctifying us, bless this offering, and graciously receive it to your altar above the skies:

Remember in your goodness and love those who have brought it, and those for whom they have brought it. Preserve us without condemnation in the service of your divine mysteries. Hallowed and glorified is your all-honored and great name, Father, and Son, and Holy Spirit, now and ever, and to all eternity.

Next the priest says:

Peace be to all.

And the deacon says to the priest:

Sir, pronounce the blessing.

Then the priest says:
Blessed be God, who blesses and sanctifies us all at the presentation of the divine and pure mysteries, and gives rest to the blessed souls among the holy and just, now and always, and to all eternity.

The deacon instructs:
Let us attend in wisdom.

The priest begins:
I believe in one God, Father Almighty, Maker of heaven and earth, and in one Lord Jesus Christ, the Son of God: *and the rest of the Creed.*

Then he bows:
God and Sovereign of all, lover of mankind, make us, who are unworthy, worthy of this hour. Being pure from all deceit and all hypocrisy, we may be united with one another by the bond of peace and love and confirmed by the sanctification of your divine knowledge through your only-begotten Son, our Lord and Savior Jesus Christ, with whom you are blessed, together with your all-holy, good, and life-giving Spirit, now and ever, and to all eternity. Amen.

The deacon instructs:
Let us stand well, let us stand reverently, let us stand in the fear of God, and with compunction of heart. In peace let us pray to the Lord.

The priest says:
For God of peace, mercy, love, and compassion, and loving-kindness are you, and your only-begotten Son, and your all-holy Spirit, now and ever.

And the people respond:
Amen.

Then the priest says:
Peace be to all.

And the people respond:
And to your spirit.

The "holy kiss" would not have been shared across genders.

The deacon instructs:
Let us greet one another with a holy kiss. Let us bow our heads to the Lord.

The priest bows and prays privately:

Only Lord and merciful God, on those who are bowing their necks before your holy altar and seeking the spiritual gifts that come from you, send forth your good grace. Bless us all with every spiritual blessing, which cannot be taken from us, you, who dwell on high, and have regard for things that are lowly.

Then the priest prays aloud:

For worthy of praise and worship and most glorious is your all-holy name, Father, Son, and Holy Spirit, now and always, and to all eternity.

The deacon says to the priest:

Sir, pronounce the blessing.

And the priest says:

The Lord will bless us, and minister with us all by his grace and loving-kindness.

The Lord will bless us, and make us worthy to stand at his holy altar, at all times, now and always, and for ever.

Blessed be God, who blesses and sanctifies us all in our attendance upon, and service of, his pure mysteries, now and always, and for ever.

The deacon instructs:

In peace, let us pray to the Lord.

And the people respond:

O Lord, have mercy.

The deacon further instructs:

Save us, have mercy on us. Pity and keep us, O God, by your grace.

For the peace that is from above, and the loving-kindness of God, and the salvation of our souls:

> Let us pray to the Lord.

For the peace of the whole world and the unity of all the holy churches of God:

> Let us pray to the Lord.

For those who bear fruit, and labor honorably in the holy churches of God, for those who remember the poor, the widows and the orphans, the strangers and needy ones, and for those who have requested us to mention them in our prayers:

> Let us pray to the Lord.

Most prayers in ancient worship rested on remembering God's activity. (Note in most prayers how strong verbs are attributed to God.) One big exception is this sort of intercessory prayer in which a deacon bids the congregation to pray for a variety of needs.

For those who are in old age and infirmity, for the sick and suffering, and those who are troubled by unclean spirits, for their speedy cure from God and their salvation:
    Let us pray to the Lord.

For those who are passing their days in virginity, celibacy, and discipline, and for those in holy matrimony; and for the holy fathers and brothers agonizing in mountains, dens, and caves of the earth:
    Let us pray to the Lord.

For Christians sailing, traveling, living among strangers, and for our brothers and sisters in captivity, in exile, in prison, and in bitter slavery, their peaceful return:
    Let us pray to the Lord.

For the remission of our sins, forgiveness of our transgressions, and for our deliverance from all tribulation, wrath, danger, and constraint, and uprising against us of enemies:
    Let us pray to the Lord.

For favorable weather, peaceful showers, beneficent dews, abundance of fruits, the perfect close of a good season, and for the crown of the year:
    Let us pray to the Lord.

For our fathers and brothers present, and praying with us in this holy hour, and at every season, their zeal, labor, and earnestness:
    Let us pray to the Lord.

For every Christian soul in tribulation and distress, and needing the mercy and succor of God; for the return of the erring, the health of the sick, the deliverance of the captives, the rest of the fathers and brothers that have fallen asleep before now:
    Let us pray to the Lord.

For the hearing and acceptance of our prayer before God, and the sending down on us his rich mercies and compassion:
    Let us pray to the Lord.

And for the offered, precious, heavenly, unutterable, pure, glorious, divine gifts, and the salvation of the priest who stands by and offers them:
    Let us offer supplication to God the Lord.

The people repeat three times:

O Lord, have mercy.

Then the priest makes the sign of the cross on the gifts, stands, and repeats three times:

Glory to God in the highest, and on earth peace, good-will among men. . . .

Next the priest repeats three times:

Lord, you will open my lips, and my mouth shall show forth your praise.

Finally the priest repeats three times:

Let my mouth be filled with your praise, O Lord, that I may tell of your glory, of your majesty, all the day.

Of the Father. Amen.

And of the Son. Amen.

And of the Holy Spirit. Amen.

Now and always, and to all eternity. Amen.

And bowing to this side and to that, the priest says:

Magnify the Lord with me, and let us exalt his name together.

The people bow and answer:

The Holy Spirit shall come upon you, and the power of the Highest shall overshadow you.

Then the priest, at great length, says privately:

O Sovereign Lord, who has visited us in compassion and mercies and has freely given to us, your humble, sinful, and unworthy servants, boldness to stand at your holy altar and to offer to you this bloodless sacrifice for our sins, the errors of the people. Look upon me, your unprofitable servant, and blot out my transgressions for your compassion's sake. Purify my lips and heart from all pollution of flesh and spirit. Remove from me every shameful and foolish thought. Fit me by the power of your all-holy Spirit for this service, and receive me graciously by your good-ness as I approach your altar.

And be pleased, O Lord, that these gifts brought by our hands may be acceptable, stooping to my weakness. Cast me not away from your presence, and abhor not my unworthiness. Pity me according to your great mercy, and according to the multitude of your mercies pass by my transgressions, that, having come before your glory without condemnation, I may be counted worthy of the protection of your only-begotten Son and of the illumination of your all-holy

Spirit, that I may not be as a slave of sin cast out, but as your servant may find grace, mercy, and forgiveness of sins before you, both in the world that now is and in that which is to come.

I pray to you, Almighty Sovereign, all-powerful Lord, hear my prayer. You are he who works all in all, and we seek in all things the help and succor that come from you and your only-begotten Son, and the good and life-giving and consubstantial Spirit, now and ever.

O God, who through your great and unspeakable love sent forth your only-begotten Son into the world in order that he might turn back the lost sheep, turn not away us sinners, laying hold of you by this bloodless sacrifice, for we trust not in our own righteousness, but in your good mercy, by which you purchased our race.

We ask for your goodness that it may be not for condemnation to your people that this mystery for salvation has been administered by us, but for remission of sins, for renewal of souls and bodies, for the well-pleasing of you, God and Father, in the mercy and love of your only-begotten Son, with whom you are blessed, together with your all-holy, good, and life-giving Spirit, now and always, and for ever.

O Lord God, who created us and brought us into life, who has shown to us the way to salvation, who has granted us a revelation of heavenly mysteries, and has appointed us to this ministry in the power of your all-holy Spirit, grant, O Sovereign, that we may become servants of your new testament, ministers of your pure mysteries. Receive us as we draw near to your holy altar, according to the greatness of your mercy, that we may become worthy of offering to you gifts and sacrifices for our transgressions and for those of the people. Allow us, O Lord, with all fear and a pure conscience to offer to you this spiritual and bloodless sacrifice, and graciously receive it to your holy and spiritual altar above the skies for an odor of a sweet spiritual smell. Send down in answer on us the grace of your all-holy Spirit.

And, O God, look upon us, and have regard to this our reasonable service, and accept it, as you accepted the gifts of Abel, the sacrifices of Noah, the priestly offices of Moses and Aaron, the peace offerings of Samuel, the repentance of David, and the incense of Zacharias. As you accepted from the hand of your apostles this true service, so accept also in your goodness from the hands of us sinners these offered gifts. Grant that our offering may be acceptable, sanctified by the Holy Spirit, as a propitiation for our transgressions and the errors of the people and for the rest of the souls that have fallen asleep before now. May we also, your humble, sinful, and unworthy servants, being counted worthy without guile to serve your holy altar, receive the reward of faithful and wise stewards, and may we find grace and mercy in the terrible day of your just and good retribution.

We thank you, O Lord our God, that you have given us boldness for the entrance of your holy places, which you have renewed to us as a new and living way through the veil of the flesh of your Christ. We, therefore, being counted worthy to enter into the place of the tabernacle of your glory, to be within the veil, and to behold the Holy of Holies, cast ourselves down before your goodness.

Remembering God's activity is a foundational practice in Christian praying, derived from Jewish roots. Of course, Christians interpreted God's saving activity from the viewpoint of Jesus Christ, as shown here. For biblical examples, see Ephesians 1:3ff. and Acts 4:24-30.

Where can we find the language to describe what God has achieved for us through Jesus Christ, particularly as experienced in the Lord's Supper? This part of

Lord, have mercy on us. Since we are full of fear and trembling, when about to stand at your holy altar and to offer this bloodless sacrifice for our own sins and for the errors of the people, send forth, O God, your good grace and sanctify our souls, bodies, and spirits. Turn our thoughts to holiness that with a pure conscience we may bring to you a peace-offering, the sacrifice of praise.

Then the priest prays aloud:
By the mercy and loving-kindness of your only-begotten Son, with whom you are blessed, together with your all-holy and good and life-giving Spirit, now and always.

And the people respond:
Amen.

Next the priest says:
Peace be to all.

And the deacon instructs:
Let us stand reverently. Let us stand in the fear of God with contrition. Let us attend to the Holy Communion service to offer peace to God.

The people respond:
The offering of peace, the sacrifice of praise.

As a veil is withdrawn from the oblation of bread and wine, the priest says:
And, uncovering the veils that darkly invest in symbol this sacred ceremonial, you reveal it clearly to us. Fill our intellectual vision with absolute light, and having purified our poverty from every pollution of flesh and spirit, make it worthy of this awe-inspiring approach. You are an all-merciful and gracious God, and we send up the praise and the thanksgiving to you, Father, Son, and Holy Spirit, now and always, and for ever.

The Anaphora is now repeated. (See the preceding section for the text of this prayer.)

The deacon says:
For the remission of our sins and the propitiation of our souls, for every soul in tribulation and distress, needing the mercy and succor of God, and for the return of the erring, the healing of the sick, the deliverance of the captives, the rest of our fathers and brothers, who have fallen asleep previously, let us all say fervently, Lord, have mercy.

the liturgy uses Old Testament images of the Tabernacle and the Temple, where a veil hid God's presence from the people to indicate how Christ has opened a way into God's glory. His body (this "flesh"), received in the sacrament, is now a new veil which no longer restricts our access and hides God's presence but opens a way for us to approach God and worship. Thus the church can offer up a sacrifice to God. The removal of the covering from the Communion elements immediately following reinforces the idea that God now is revealed through Jesus Christ.

To speak of the "oblation" of bread and wine is to draw from the ancient notion that the Lord's Supper is not only something Christians receive but also something they offer to God in praise and thanksgiving. Notice how the anaphora of St. James speaks of offering to God "an awesome and bloodless sacrifice" in light of God's compassion, and how Egeria regularly spoke of the Eucharist as the Offering.

In response, the people repeat twelve times:
Lord, have mercy.

Next the priest breaks the bread, holds half in his right hand and the other half in his left, and dips that in his right hand in a chalice, saying:
The union of the all-holy body and precious blood of our Lord and God and Savior, Jesus Christ.

Then he makes the sign of the cross on the piece which is in his left hand. And then with his left hand he signs the piece now held in his right hand and says:
Behold the Lamb of God, the Son of the Father, who takes away the sins of the world, sacrificed for the life and salvation of the world.

Then he begins to divide the Eucharistic bread before all, making sure he gives a single piece to each chalice, saying:
It has been made one, sanctified, and perfected in the name of the Father, of the Son, and of the Holy Spirit, now and ever.

And when he gives a single piece to each chalice, he also says:
A holy portion of Christ, full of grace and truth, of the Father and of the Holy Spirit, to whom be the glory and the power to all eternity.

As he is dividing, he says:
The Lord is my Shepherd; I shall not want. In green pastures, . . .

I will bless the Lord at all times . . .

O praise the Lord, all you nations . . .

Next the deacon says to the priest:
Sir, pronounce the blessing.

The priest says:
The Lord will bless us and keep us without condemnation for the communion of his pure gifts, now and always, and for ever.

And when they have filled the chalices, the deacon says:
Sir, pronounce the blessing.

The priest says:

The Lord will bless us, and make us worthy with the pure touching of our fingers to take the live coal and place it upon the mouths of the faithful for the purification and renewal of their souls and bodies, now and always.

O taste and see that the Lord is good. The Lord is parted and not divided, distributed to the faithful but not expended, for the remission of sins and the life everlasting now and always, and for ever.

The deacon says:

In the peace of Christ, let us sing.

The singers respond:

O taste and see that the Lord is good.

Next the priest says the prayer before the communion:

O Lord our God, the heavenly bread, the life of the universe, I have sinned against heaven and before you. I am not worthy to partake of your pure mysteries. As a merciful God, make me worthy by your grace, without condemnation, to partake of your holy body and precious blood for the remission of sins and life everlasting.

In this ancient liturgy, like others from the time, the worthiness to participate in Communion itself is a gift of God, not a human accomplishment. Compare Colossians 1:12.

Then the priest distributes to the clergy.

When the deacons take the plates and the chalices for distribution to the people, the deacon, who takes the first plate, says to the priest:

Sir, pronounce the blessing.

The priest says:

Glory to God, who has sanctified and is sanctifying us all.

The deacon says:

Be exalted, O God, over the heavens, and your glory be over all the earth. Your kingdom endures to all eternity.

And when the deacon is about to put the Eucharistic vessels on the side table, the priest says:

Blessed be the name of the Lord our God for ever.

The deacon instructs the people:

In the fear of God, and in faith and love, draw nigh.

The people respond:
Blessed is he that comes in the name of the Lord.

And again, when the deacon sets down the plate upon the side table, he says to the priest:
Sir, pronounce the blessing.

The priest says:
Save your people, O God, and bless your inheritance. Glory to our God, who has sanctified us all.

And when he has put the chalice back on the holy table, the priest says:
Blessed be the name of the Lord to all eternity.

The deacons and the people say together:
Fill our mouths with your praise, O Lord, and fill our lips with joy, that we may sing of your glory, of your greatness all the day.

We render thanks to you, Christ our God, that you have made us worthy to partake of your body and blood, for the remission of sins, and for life everlasting. In your goodness and love, keep us, we pray, without condemnation.

We give thanks to you, the Savior and God of all, for all the good things you have given us, and for the participation of your holy and pure mysteries. We offer to you this incense, praying: "Keep us under the shadow of your wings, and count us worthy till our last breath to partake of your holy rites for the sanctification of our souls and bodies, for the inheritance of the kingdom of heaven. You, O God, are our sanctification, and we send up praise and thanksgiving to you, Father, Son, and Holy Spirit."

The deacon says at the start of another procession:
Glory to you, glory to you, glory to you, O Christ the King, only-begotten Word of the Father, that you have counted us, your sinful and unworthy servants, worthy to enjoy your pure mysteries for the remission of sins, and for life everlasting: glory to you.

And when the procession is completed, the deacon says:
Again and again, and at all times, in peace, let us pray to the Lord.

That the participation in his holy rites may be to us for the turning away from every wicked thing, for our support on the journey to life everlasting, for the communion and gift of the Holy Spirit: let us pray.

The priest says:
Commemorating our all-holy, pure, most glorious, blessed Lady, the God-Mother and Ever-Virgin Mary, and all the saints that have been well-pleasing to you since the world began, let us devote ourselves, and one another, and our whole life, to Christ our God:

Throughout the liturgy of St. James, the use of incense is a recurring element with several symbolic meanings. Interestingly, it does not appear in Egeria's description of Jerusalem's worship. This discrepancy is likely one of those omissions in her diary so frustrating to modern historians. Why didn't she mention it? Was it because using incense did not strike her as unusual, because she did not notice when it was used, or because its use was less frequent in the earlier stages of Jerusalem's liturgy? It is difficult to say with certainty.

Such attention to Mary in the liturgy is likely an addition made after the fourth century.

And the people respond:

To you, O Lord.

The priest says:

O God, who through your great and unspeakable love did condescend to the weakness of your servants and has counted us worthy to partake of this heavenly table, condemn not us sinners for the participation of your pure mysteries. But keep us, O good One, in the sanctification of your Holy Spirit, that, being made holy, we may find part and inheritance with all your saints that have been well-pleasing to you since the world began, in the light of your countenance, through the mercy of your only-begotten Son, our Lord and God and Savior Jesus Christ, with whom you are blessed, together with your all-holy, good, and life-giving Spirit. Blessed and glorified is your all-precious and glorious name, Father, Son, and Holy Spirit, now and ever, and to all eternity.

And the people respond:

Amen.

The priest says:

Peace be to all.

And the people respond:

And to your spirit.

The deacon instructs:

Let us bow our heads to the Lord.

The priest prays privately:

O God, great and marvelous, look upon your servants, for we have bowed our heads to you. Stretch forth your hand, strong and full of blessings, and bless your people. Keep your inheritance, that always and at all times we may glorify you, our only living and true God, the holy and consubstantial Trinity, Father, Son, and Holy Ghost, now and ever, and to all eternity.

Then the priest prays aloud:

For to you is due praise from us, and honor, adoration, and thanksgiving, Father, Son, and Holy Spirit, now and ever.

The deacon says:

In the peace of Christ, let us sing.
In the peace of Christ, let us go on.

And the people respond:

In the name of the Lord. Sir, pronounce the blessing.

Then the deacon offers the prayer of dismissal:

Going on from glory to glory, we praise you, the Savior of our souls. Glory to Father, and Son, and Holy Spirit now and ever, and to all eternity. We praise you, the Savior of our souls.

The priest says a prayer from the altar to the sacristy:

Going on from strength to strength, and having fulfilled all the divine service in your temple, even now we pray to you, O Lord our God, make us worthy of perfect loving-kindness. Make straight our path. Root us in your fear, and make us worthy of the heavenly kingdom in Christ Jesus our Lord, with whom you are blessed, together with your all-holy, good, and life-giving Spirit, now and always, and for ever.

The view from the Communion table looks upward to the heavenly realm and outward to Christian faithfulness in the world and ultimately to the coming Kingdom of God, not just backward to the Last Supper.

The deacon prays:

Again and again, and at all times, in peace let us pray to the Lord.

You have given us, O Lord, sanctification in the communion of the all-holy body and precious blood of your only-begotten Son, our Lord Jesus Christ. Give to us also the grace of your good Spirit, and keep us blameless in the faith. Lead us to perfect adoption and redemption and to the coming joys of eternity, for you are our sanctification and light, O God, and your only-begotten Son, and your all-holy Spirit, now and ever, and to all eternity. Amen.

The deacon instructs:

In the peace of Christ, let us keep watch.

Then the priest offers the final prayer:

Blessed is God, who blesses and sanctifies us through the communion of the holy, life-giving, and pure mysteries, now and ever, and to all eternity. Amen.

O Lord Jesus Christ, Son of the living God, Lamb and Shepherd, who takes away the sin of the world, who freely forgave the debt of the two debtors and gave remission of sins to the woman that was a sinner, who gave healing to the paralytic with the remission of his sins, forgive, remit, pardon, O God, our offenses, voluntary and involuntary, in knowledge and in ignorance, by transgression and by disobedience, which your all-holy Spirit knows better than your servants do.

And if humanity, carnal and dwelling in this world, have in anything erred from your commandments, either moved by the devil, whether in word or in deed, or if they have come under a curse, or by reason of some special vow, I entreat and ask your unspeakable loving-kindness, that they may be set free from their word and released from the oath and the special vow, according to your goodness.

Truly, O Sovereign Lord, hear my supplication on behalf of your servants, and pass by all their errors, remembering them no more. Forgive them every transgression, voluntary and involuntary. Deliver them from everlasting punishment, for you are he that has commanded us, saying, "Whatsoever things you bind upon earth, shall be bound in heaven. Whatsoever things you loose upon earth, shall be loosed in heaven." You are our God, a God able to pity, to save, and to forgive sins. Glory is due you, with the eternal Father, and the life-giving Spirit, now and ever, and to all eternity. Amen.

Source: The liturgy of St. James is adapted from volume 7 of *The Ante-Nicene Fathers: Translations of the Writings of the Fathers down to A.D. 325,* edited by Alexander Roberts and James Donaldson (Grand Rapids: Wm. B. Eerdmans Pub. Co., 1951), pp. 537-50. There are two manuscripts of the Greek liturgy of St. James, one from the tenth and one from the twelfth centuries, as well as fragments from a third. The first edition appeared in Rome in 1526. The liturgy of St. James has been edited by William Trollope [*The Greek Liturgy of St. James,* edited and with an English introduction and notes, together with a Latin version of the Syriac copy, and the Greek text restored to its original purity and accompanied by a literal English translation (Edinburgh: T&T Clark, 1848)], John Mason Neale [*Tetralogia Liturgica* (London, 1849) and *Liturgies of St. Mark, St. James, St. Clement, St. Chrysostom, and St. Basil,* second ed. (London, 1868)], and Hermann Daniel [*Codex Liturgicus* (Hildesheim, 1846)]. Bishop Thomas Rattray attempted to separate the original from the interpolations in *The Ancient Liturgy of the Church of Jerusalem* (London, 1744). Christian Karl Josias Freiherr von Bunsen tried to restore the Anaphora to its fourth-century state in the third volume of his *Analecta Ante-Nicaena* (London: Longman, Brown, Green, and Longmans, 1854). The standard critical edition in Greek (with Latin translation) is B. C. Mercier, *La Liturgie de S. Jacques, Patrologia Orientalis* 26, 2 (Paris: Firmin-Didot, 1946).

Sermons

Cyril's Sermon on the Story of the Paralytic by the Pool

The following sermon on John 5:2-15 was preached by Cyril while he was still a presbyter, not yet bishop of Jerusalem. The sermon reflects early church ways of handling Scripture in sermons: the Incarnate God is the key to salvation, and the entirety of Scripture witnesses to his saving work. The numbering below reflects the scholarly practice of identifying different parts of a historic piece. The numbers from the source for these sermons have been replicated.

1   Wherever Jesus appears, there also is salvation. If he sees a tax collector seated at the counter, he makes him an apostle and an evangelist. If he is buried among the dead, he raises them. He gives sight to the blind and hearing to the deaf. When he walks around the pools, it is not to inspect the buildings but to heal the sick.

2   In Jerusalem there used to be a sheep pool with five porticos—four surrounding the pool, the fifth in the middle—where there lay a great crowd of the sick. There was much unbelief among the Jews. The Physician and Nurse of souls and bodies granted healing in due order. First he tended the man who had long been sick so that he might experience the speediest release from his sufferings. This man had been lying there not for a day or two, or even a month or a year, but for thirty-eight years. Having become well-known to the onlookers in the course of his lengthy illness, he was able to display the power of the healer, for everyone knew him because of the length of time he had been paralyzed. Though the Supreme Physician was revealing his power, he was despised by those who took it wrongly.

3   As Jesus walked round the pool, he saw. He didn't learn by asking questions: his divine power supplied what was lacking. He saw, without asking, how long the man had been lying there. His eyes taught him what he already knew before he saw it. With regard to what was in the heart, he had no need to ask anyone about the man, for he knew for himself what was in man (cf. John 2:25; 16:30). All the more was this true with regard to diseases which come from outside.

4   He saw a man lying under the weight of a severe illness, for he carried a great burden of sins, and the suffering brought on by his illness had been prolonged. Jesus' question to him somehow expressed what he had been longing to hear: "Do you want to be healed?" That

Consider how quickly Cyril makes a strong statement about Christ's saving activity. Contrast his approach to many forms of current preaching that take time to move into the Gospel. How long should it take before Gospel content begins to appear in a sermon?

The idea that Jesus Christ is not only human but also divine is never far from Cyril's mind. Acknowledging the divinity of Christ leads Cyril to offer a "theological" reading of the events in Christ's ministry: this is God who is acting.

was all he said, and broke off in the middle of the question. The question had two meanings: the disease was of the soul as well as of the body. This is shown by Jesus' following remark: "See, you have been cured. Do not sin any more, so that nothing worse happens to you." That is why he asked him: "Do you want to be healed?" Observe the healer's great skill. He makes the cure depend upon the desire. It is because salvation comes from faith that the man was asked "Do you want?" so that the desire might prepare the way for the miracle. No one but Jesus spoke in this way, not even the best of earthly doctors, for doctors who treat earthly diseases cannot say, "Do you want to be healed?" to all their patients. But Jesus gives even the desire. He accepts the faith and grants the favor without a fee.

5 Once our Savior was walking along the road where two blind men were sitting. However, while physically they were blind, their minds still enjoyed the power of vision. Though the scribes did not recognize Jesus, the blind men's cries pointed him out. Even though the Pharisees had learned the law and practiced it from childhood to old age, they had become unteachable in their advanced years. Referring to Jesus, they declared, "We don't know where he comes from" (John 9:29). This was not surprising, for "he came into his own, and his own did not accept him" (John 1:11). The blind, on the other hand, cried out, "Son of David, have pity on us" (cf. Mark 10:47). The one whom the learned lawyers did not recognize was recognized by those who could not see.

The Savior went up to them and said, "Do you believe that I can do this?" (Matthew 9:28). "What do you want me to do for you?" (Matthew 20.32). He did not say, "What do you want me to say to you?"; instead, he said, "What do you want me to do for you?" He was the creator and the giver of life; his creative power was not something new. His Father is always at work (cf. John 5:17), and he works alongside his Father. He was creator of all things by his Father's decree. He, who is the only-begotten of the only God without intermediary, asks the blind men: "What do you want me to do for you?" Not that he didn't know what they wanted, for the truth was plain to see. But he intended the gift to follow from their own words, so that by their own words they might be justified. It is not to be supposed that the one who knows hearts doesn't know what they would say, but by waiting for them to speak, he let their request elicit the miracle.

6 So Jesus approached the sick man. Uninvited, the doctor visited the patient. It should not surprise us that he visited the man lying by the pool, since he came down to us uninvited from heaven. "Do you want to be cured?" he asked him. With this question he led him on to knowledge and aroused him to question in his turn. This was a great and gracious gift. He could not pay the fee, so he had a voluntary healer. "Yes, Lord," he replied. "My years of suffering have made me long for health. I do long for it, but I have no man [to help me into the pool]."

This idea of being able to see truly is a recurring one in preaching at the time. Here Cyril applies it to correct perception of Jesus. Elsewhere he will speak of being able to discern rightly the power of God in the church's sacraments.

Cyril's preaching of this biblical episode is profoundly theological. The paralytic doesn't find just a man to help him; he encounters the one who is both God and human, God incarnate. The pool becomes irrelevant for his healing in the light of the Incarnation.

Do not be downcast, my friend, because you have no man. You have God standing beside you, who is in one respect man, in another God, for we must profess both truths. To acknowledge his humanity without acknowledging his divinity is useless, or rather brings a curse, for "Cursed is he who places his hope in a man" (Jeremiah 17:5). So if we place our hope even in Jesus as a man without involving his divinity in our hope, we incur a curse. But as it is, we acknowledge him to be both God and human, and both in literal truth. As the one begotten of a true Father, and as a man born in truth and not in mere appearance, we adore him and look forward to a true salvation.

7   "I want to be cured, but I have no man." Can't you see that at the very point where the remedy is lacking, he has given you the miracle? For while most of the sick had houses and relations and perhaps other people too, he suffered complete and utter poverty. When he had no help from outside to support him and was left totally to his own resources, God's only-begotten son came to his help. "Do you want to be healed?" "Yes, Lord, but I have no man to put me into the pool when the water is disturbed." You have the fountain, for "with you is the fountain of life" (Psalm 36:9), the fountain which is the source of all fountains. "If anyone drinks from this water, streams of living water will flow within him" (John 7:38), not water that flows downwards, but water that "springs up" (John 4:14). Jesus' water does not make us leap down from above but leap up from earthly things to heavenly. This water "springs up to eternal life," for Jesus is the source of blessings.

8   Why do you linger round a pool? You are the one who walked on the waters, who rebuked the winds, who controlled the sea, the one beneath whom the sea was spread like a floor, and who gave Peter the same power to walk on it. When there was no glimmer in the night, the light was there, unrecognized. As he walked on the waters, no one recognized him by glimpsing his face, but the familiar voice revealed his presence. Thinking they saw a ghost, they were terrified. But Jesus said to them, "It is I. Do not be afraid." "If you are the one I know," Peter replied, "or rather the one whom the Father has revealed to me, tell me to come to you across the waters." "Come," said Jesus, generous in sharing his gifts.

9   So the one who controlled and created the waters was there beside the water of the pool. "I have no man," the paralytic said to him, "to put me into the pool when the water is disturbed." "Why are you waiting for the waters to be disturbed?" the Savior said to him. "Do not be disturbed; be healed." Why are you waiting for a visible movement? The word of command is swifter than thought. Simply look at the power of the spring and recognize God appearing in the flesh. Do not judge by his appearance, but by the work which he accomplishes through the appearance. "I have no man to put me into the pool when the

Cyril's sermon never allows the spotlight to drift from Jesus Christ, who he is and what he has done. As Christ is the key to interpreting the whole breadth of salvation history, he is also the key to understanding Scripture, human need and God's provision for it, and ultimately, God the Father himself.

water is disturbed." "Why do you wait for what is trivial?" Jesus said to him. Why look for healing in the waters? Rise up, the Resurrection has told you. For the Savior is everything for everyone everywhere: bread for the hungry, water for the thirsty, resurrection for the dead, a physician for the sick, redemption for the sinner.

10   Stand up, pick up your mattress, and walk. But first stand up; first cast off your disease. Then recover the sinew of faith. First lean on the mattress which is supporting you. Then learn to use a wooden frame to carry the things which have long carried you. This same Savior ordered you to carry the wooden palanquin of which it is said: "King Solomon made himself a litter from the wood of Lebanon. He made its posts of silver, its back of gold, its seat of purple; its interior was inlaid with stones" (Song of Songs 3:9-10). Symbols of the passion are hidden away in these songs, which are bridal, sober, and chaste. Do not interpret these words obtusely as many have done, taking them to be passionate love songs. They are bridal words, full of modesty.

However, if you are not familiar with the Canticle, turn to the Proverbs, and make your way up to the Canticle gradually. "Wisdom has built for herself a house" (the text speaks of Wisdom as a woman) "and sent out her servants" (Proverbs 9:1, 3). In another place it says: "Love her, and she will protect you" (Proverbs 4:6). This is not love of a woman, but of wisdom, which drives out carnal passion. Where wisdom is gained, passion is banished. Passions do not accord with wisdom, but wise thoughts do. Passion makes men like lusting stallions; their craving knows no reason. So if you hear the Canticle apparently speaking of a bridegroom and a bride, do not descend to understand the words in an erotic sense, but exercise yourself in passionless thoughts as a means of transforming your passions.

Ultimately, like other patristic preachers, Cyril believes all Scriptures speak to the Gospel of Jesus Christ. Rather than treat passages or books as isolated entities, reading in and out of them, Cyril will treat Scripture as an integrative whole of Christian salvation history and read across Scriptures. The Jerusalem lectionary did the same.

11   Meditate, then, on the sacred lessons of the Canticle, for they are expressions of chastity and tell of Christ's Passion. They reveal the details of his passion. They tell us the place: "He has come into the garden" (cf. Song of Songs 5:1), for that is where he was buried. They recalled the spices: "He has taken the fullness of my myrrh" (cf. Song of Songs 5:5), for his human life has been completed. And after the resurrection he said: "I have eaten my bread with my honey" (Song of Songs 5:1), for "they gave him a piece of honeycomb" (Luke 24:42, variant). The Canticle spoke also of the wine mixed with myrrh: "I shall give you spiced wine to drink" (Song of Songs 8:2). In another passage they spoke of the myrrh which was poured on his head: "While the king was on his couch, my nard gave out its perfume" (Song of Songs 1:12), for "as he sat at table in the house of Simon the Leper, a woman came in and broke open an alabaster jar of very costly ointment of pure nard and poured it on his head" (Mark 14:3).

So too with regard to the cross. The "litter" refers to the wood of the cross on which he was carried. "He has made its posts of silver": the beginning of the cross is of silver, namely, the betrayal. Just as a luxurious house is crowned with a golden roof and has pillars to support the whole edifice, so too silver was the beginning of his crucifixion and resurrection. If Judas had not betrayed him, he would not have been crucified. For this reason he made his pillars of silver as the beginning of his renowned Passion.

12   "Its seat of purple." And so they dressed him in purple, partly in mockery, partly prophetically, for he was a king. Though they were acting mainly for their own amusement, still they did it, and it was a sign of his royal dignity. And though his crown was of thorns, it was a crown, and woven by soldiers, for kings are proclaimed by their soldiers. "Its seat of purple, its interior paved with stones." Well-instructed members of the church know of Lithostrotos, also called Gabbatha, in Pilate's house.

Lithostrotos and *Gabbatha* are the Greek and Aramaic words for "paved with stones." See John 19:13.

13   In explaining this I have digressed from the mattress to the litter. Well then, Jesus said to the man: "Stand up, pick up your mattress, and walk." The disease had been protracted, but the treatment was instantaneous. For years the sinews had been paralyzed, yet instantaneously they were restored. The very creator of the sinews was here, the one who contrived various cures for the blind, who used a salve of mud to dispense a miraculous remedy. If mud is applied to a man who can see, it impedes his vision, but Jesus used mud to give sight to the blind. In other cases Jesus used other means to exercise his healing power; in this case by the words: "Stand up, pick up your mattress, and walk."

Imagine the onlookers' amazement. Given the wonderful sight, their lack of faith was strange. The long-term disease was cured, but the long-lasting incredulity was not. The Jews remained ill and had no desire to be cured.

14   If they marveled at the event, they should have also worshiped the healer of souls and bodies. But they grumbled, for grumbling ran in their family. They inverted good and evil, calling bitter sweet and sweet bitter.

With full deliberation Jesus used to work on the Sabbath. He did works that transcended the Sabbath in order to teach a lesson by the very act of working. Since one argument defeats another but action is invincible, he gave an object lesson by healing on the Sabbath. Thus, he did not pit argument against argument but used the work to persuade the onlookers.

15   "It is the Sabbath," they said. "It is not lawful for you to carry your mattress." Although the Lawgiver himself was present, he was not the one who said: "It is not lawful." The text "Appoint, O Lord, a lawgiver against them" (Psalm 9:20) refers to the Savior. They were at

once answered by the man who had just been healed in soul and body. Wisdom lent him wise words; though unable to answer in legal terms, his reply was concise.

"You are all aware," he said, "how long I have been ill, how many years I have been bed-ridden and how helpless my case has been. Not one of you ever did me the service of lifting me up and putting me first in the pool to be cured. So when you have done nothing to help me, why do you now act like lawyers and say: 'It is not lawful for you to carry your mattress on the Sabbath'?

"I can answer you very briefly: the man who cured me told me to do it. You may think nothing of me, but the event should leave you dumbfounded. He put no ointment on me; he employed no medical techniques or aids. He simply spoke, and the effect followed. He gave me an order, and I am obeying it. I trust his command because his command healed me. If the man who gave me the order hadn't the power to heal me by his orders, it would not be right for me to obey them. But since my illness, which for many years has been plain to see, has ceased at his command, it is right for me to listen to him, seeing that my illness has listened to him and departed. It was the man who restored my health who said to me: 'Pick up your mattress.'"

16   The man who was healed did not know who his Healer was. We can see how far our Savior was from vainglory. Having worked the cure, he slipped away, not wanting to receive credit for the cure. We do just the opposite. If we ever experience dreams, perform works of healing with our hands, or drive away demons by an invocation, we are so far from hiding our success that we boast of it even before we are questioned. Jesus teaches us by his own example not to speak about ourselves. Once the cure was provided, he slipped away so as not to receive the credit. He withdrew at the right time and came back at the right time. In order to set healing of the soul alongside the physical cure, he came once the crowd had dispersed, and said, "See, you are cured. Do not sin anymore."

Notice what is not in Cyril's sermon, especially long personal anecdotes. Are anecdotes necessary for the faithful preaching of the Gospel?

17   What a versatile healer! Sometimes he heals the soul before the body, sometimes vice versa. "Do not sin anymore, in case something worse happens to you." This one example contains a general lesson, for the words apply not only to that one man, but to us all. If ever we suffer illness or grief or hardship, we should not blame God. "For God cannot be tempted with evil, nor does he himself tempt anyone" (James 1:13). Each of us [is] "caught in the ropes of his own sin" (Proverbs 5.22) and scourged.

"Do not sin anymore so that nothing worse happens to you." Let all mankind attend to these words. Now let the fornicator set aside his lust. Now let the miser turn almsgiver. Now let the thief heed the words, "Do not sin anymore."

God's forgiveness is great, his grace generous. But do not let the vastness of his mercy lead you to presumption or make his forbearance a reason for sin. Rather, let your carnal passions in future be healed. Make your own the words of the reading which suit your case so well: "For while we were in the flesh, our sinful passions which came through the law were active in our members" (Romans 7:5). When the apostle said, "While we were in the flesh," he was not speaking of the flesh which clothes us but of our carnal actions. For when he said, "While we were in the flesh," he was still clothed in flesh himself. But just as God said before bringing about the flood, "My spirit shall not remain in these people because they are flesh" (Genesis 6:3), for the spirit had been transformed into carnal desire, in the same sense the apostle [said], "While we were in the flesh" in this passage.

18   So no one should be in the flesh, or rather, while in the flesh we should not "walk according to the flesh" (Romans 8:4). For the apostle doesn't want us to withdraw completely from the world in order to avoid doing evil, but while remaining in the flesh to enslave the flesh and not be led by it. We should be leaders, not slaves. We should take food in moderation, and instead of being carried away by gluttony we should restrain our bellies in order to control our lower parts. Let the body be led by the soul instead of the soul being carried away by carnal pleasures.

   "Do not sin anymore so that nothing worse happens to you." These words contain a message for us all. I only wish everyone had ears to hear them. When words reach the hearing of the flesh, they are not always admitted to the mind. This is what the Savior implied when he said, "He that has ears to hear, let him hear" (Matthew 11:15), for he was speaking to people who had the ears of the flesh.

19   So let everyone listen to Jesus and avoid sin in future, running instead to the one who forgives our sins. If we are ill, let us seek refuge with him. If our spirits are afflicted, let us have recourse to the doctor of knowledge. If we are hungry, let us accept his bread. If we are dead, let us share his resurrection. If we have grown old in ignorance, let us ask Wisdom to grant us wisdom.

20   My thoughts have led me into speaking for too long. Perhaps this has impeded our Father's teaching. The hour calls us to hear great words. May they enable us to perform greater works through which to praise God, to whom is the glory now and always and for ever and ever. Amen.

Notice how this final paragraph indicates Jerusalem's practice of preaching multiple sermons in that Cyril appears concerned that he save time for his bishop's sermon to follow.

Excerpts from a Sermon Cyril Preached
to Baptismal Candidates at the Beginning of Lent

This sermon marked the beginning of the intensive preparation for baptism. Cyril preached it as bishop to steel baptismal candidates for the rigorous instruction and ascetic practices that preceded their baptism coming at Easter. The numbering below reflects the scholarly practice of identifying different parts of a historic piece. Some numbers are skipped below because only excerpts of the sermon are provided.

PROCATECHESIS
Or Prologue to the Catecheses

Enlightenment is another patristic term for baptism. It hints at the illumination one receives in the wisdom of Christ. Notice how the anticipation of Easter already flavors Cyril's understanding of these candidates standing on the threshold of Lent.

Most English translations of this verse say "according to *his* purpose," supplying what is implied in the original Greek for Romans 8:28. To emphasize the candidates' decision (i.e., purpose), Cyril supplies "their" instead.

Christians today often think of baptism in a narrow way, as an application of water. For the church in Jerusalem, baptism was a complex of events and rites of which the water was the pinnacle. Here Cyril speaks of the scriptural instruction and the cleansing prayers which preceded the application of water but were an important preparation for it.

1   Already, dear candidates for enlightenment, the scent of blessedness has come upon you. Already you are gathering spiritual flowers to weave into heavenly crowns. Already the perfume of the Holy Spirit has breathed over you. You are already outside the outer hall of the palace. I pray that the king may lead you inside. The blossom can now be seen on the trees. I pray that the fruit may follow. So far your enrollment and your call to military service have taken place. We have had the bridesmaids' lamps, a yearning for the heavenly city, good intentions, and the hope which accompanies them, for he who said "For those who love God everything works together for good" does not lie (Romans 8:28). God is a generous benefactor, but he waits for each one's decision. This is why the apostle went on to say, "to those who are called according to their purpose." It is a true purpose which makes you one of the called, for if you are here in body but not in mind, you gain nothing.

9   Be eager to attend the catechetical classes. Be earnest in submitting to the exorcisms. If you are blown upon and exorcised, the process brings you salvation. Imagine an unworked lump of gold that is adulterated and combined with a variety of other substances, like bronze, tin, iron, and lead. We are trying to get pure gold. Can the impurities be removed from it without fire? In the same way, the soul can't be purified without exorcisms. They are sacred, for they have been taken from Holy Scripture. Your face is veiled to leave your mind at rest and to prevent a wandering gaze from making your heart wander too. Though your eyes are veiled, your ears are free to receive salvation. As goldsmiths achieve their effect by directing their breath into the fire through narrow pipes and blowing on the gold hidden in the retort and stimulating the flame underneath, so too the exorcists inspire fear through the Holy Spirit and, so to speak, rekindle the soul inside the retort of the body. Our enemy the devil departs, but salvation and the hope of eternal life remain. Purified of its sins, the soul henceforth possesses salvation. So, let us persevere in hope, offer ourselves, and be hopeful so that the God of all things, seeing our intentions, may

cleanse us of our sins, inspire us with good hope of our welfare, and give us the repentance which leads to salvation. God has called; you have been called.

10 Persevere with the catechetical classes. If we have a lot to say, don't relax your attention. You are being given weapons to use against the powers ranged against you, weapons against heresies, against Jews and Samaritans and pagans. You have many enemies. Take a good supply of weapons, for you have to shoot against many adversaries. You must learn how to shoot down the Greek and how to fight against the heretic, the Jew and the Samaritan. Your arms are ready, and above all is the sword of the Spirit. You must stretch out your right hand for the good cause to fight the Lord's fight, to conquer the powers ranged against you, and to become invincible to any heretical force.

11 Let this be your order of the day: learn what you are told and keep it for ever. Do not imagine that these are ordinary homilies, which are good and deserve credence, thinking if we neglect them today, we have tomorrow to learn. The instructions on the font of rebirth are given in sequence. If they are neglected today, when will the loss be made good? Imagine it is the season for planting trees. If we haven't dug deep, when else can the tree that has once been badly planted be planted properly? Think of catechesis as if it were a house. If we don't use clamps in the right order to hold the structure together and to prevent gaps appearing, the building becomes unsound and even our earlier efforts will be wasted. Stone must follow stone, and corner fit corner in the right order. We must smooth away irregularities if the building is to rise. In the same way we bring you, so to speak, stones of knowledge. You must learn about the living God. You must learn about judgment. You must learn about Christ. You must learn about the resurrection. I shall have many things to say in order: first I must explain them point by point and only later in their mutual connections. If you don't join them together into a single whole, remembering what comes first and what second, I will have performed my task of building, but the structure you have will be unsound.

> The instruction one received prior to baptism was one of the few educational "programs" in the late patristic church. Thus Cyril is emphasizing the importance of regular attendance for his baptismal candidates in what will be one of the most critical opportunities for systematic instruction in the faith.

16 The baptism which lies before you is a matter of great importance. For prisoners it means ransom and for sinners forgiveness: the death of sin, new birth for the soul, a shining garment, a holy, indelible seal, a chariot to heaven, the food of paradise, the grant of royalty, and the grace of adoption. Nevertheless, a serpent is on the lookout for those who take this road. Do not let him bite you and infect you with unbelief. He sees so many people being saved and "seeks someone to devour" (1 Peter 5:8). You are approaching the father of spirits, but you have to pass that serpent. How will you get past? Let your feet be shod in readiness with the gospel of peace so that even if you are bitten, you will come to no harm. Have faith living within you, and sturdy hope like a strong shoe so that you can get

> For Cyril, one valid meaning does not necessarily exclude another. To highlight the awesomeness of baptism, Cyril used the technique of heaping up descriptions and effects of the sacrament.

past your enemy and reach the Lord (cf. Ephesians 6:15). Prepare your heart to welcome your instruction and to share in the holy mysteries. Pray more frequently that God may choose you to receive the heavenly, immortal mysteries. Do not be idle by day or by night. As soon as sleep falls from your eyes, let your mind be intent on prayer. If you notice any shameful thought coming to the surface of your mind, remember judgment and salvation. Concentrate your mind on receiving instruction so as to forget unworthy thoughts. If you meet anyone who says, "So you're going to go down into the water? Aren't there baths in the city anymore?," imagine that this is the sea serpent plotting against you. Pay attention not to what the person is saying, but to what God is doing. Guard your soul so as not to be caught, but to remain in hope and become an heir to eternal salvation.

Examples of the Instructions Cyril Delivered to Baptismal Candidates during Lent

Jerusalem's bishop carefully instructed those preparing for baptism in the overarching biblical story and in the key doctrines of the faith. The following excerpts from Cyril's fourth instruction to the baptismal candidates show how he handled the doctrines concerning each of the three Persons of the Trinity.

Reading: Colossians 2:8ff.: "See to it that no one takes you captive through philosophy and empty deceit, according to human tradition, according to the elemental spirits of the universe . . ."

On God

4   So to begin with, let your soul have the dogma concerning God as its foundation. There is one God, who is unique, unbegotten, without beginning or change or alteration. He was not begotten by another and has no one who will succeed to his life. He did not begin his life in time, nor will he ever end it. He is good and just. So if you ever hear a heretic saying that one God is just and another good, you will immediately remember what I say and recognize the poisoned dart. Some people have presumed in their blasphemous teaching to divide the one God. Some have distinguished between two Lords and creators, of the soul and bodies respectively — a foolish and irreverent doctrine. How can one person become the servant of two masters? The Lord says in the Gospels, "No one can serve two masters" (Matthew 6:24). God is, therefore, one and unique, the maker of both souls and bodies. The one creator of heaven and earth is also the maker of angels and archangels. Though creator of many beings, he is the eternal father of one alone, his one, only-begotten son, our Lord Jesus Christ, through whom he made all things, both visible and invisible.

> Cyril must address not only abstractions about God but also teachings circulating in the church which he considered erroneous. One such teaching sought to reconcile the seeming contradiction between God as a harsh judge in the Old Testament and as a loving Father in the New. One solution? State that the God in the Old Testament is different than the one in the New. Cyril would have none of this way of thinking.

5   He is the Father of our Lord Jesus Christ. He is not circumscribed in space or smaller than the sky. No, the heavens are the work of his fingers, and he holds the whole earth in his grasp (cf. Psalm 8:3; Isaiah 40:12). He is in everything and outside everything. Do not imagine he is smaller than the sun or its equal, for the one who made the sun ought rather to be, in the first place, incomparably greater and brighter. He foresees the future and is more powerful than anything. He knows everything and acts as he will. He is not subject to the succession of things or generation or chance or fate. In everything he is complete, and he contains equally every form of perfection. He does not grow lesser or greater but is always identical and the same. He has prepared punishment for sinners and rewards for the righteous.

There is a hint of sarcasm in noting that those who worship the sun or the moon have half a day when they have no god. Cyril's comment about Aphrodite is particularly acute, because a temple to that goddess previously stood over the site of Jesus' crucifixion and resurrection.

6   Many have strayed away from the one God in various ways. Some have made God out to be the sun so that when the sun sets, they remain godless throughout the night. Others have made him out to be the moon so that they have no God by day. Some see God as the other parts of the universe, the arts, foods, or other pleasures. Some in their lust for women set up on high the statue of a naked woman, calling it Aphrodite, and worship passion under this visible form. Others have been so smitten by the brightness of gold that they have made a god of it and of other substances. However, if from the beginning you set the teaching about God's undivided power as a foundation in your heart and believe it, you will cut out at a stroke all the corrupting evils of idolatry and heretical error. So in faith set this first doctrine of religion in your soul as a foundation.

On Christ

Cyril's comments on Jesus were particularly important because some in the fourth century spoke of a time when the Son of God did not exist (e.g., Arians) or subordinated the Son of God to God the Father.

7   Believe too in God's one and only son, our Lord Jesus Christ, who is God begotten by God, Life begotten by Life, Light begotten by Light, like in everything to the one who begot him. He did not begin in time, but was begotten by the Father before all ages, eternally and inconceivably. He is God's wisdom, power, and justice in substantial form. He has been seated at the Father's right hand before all ages. He was not crowned after his Passion, as some have imagined, as if he received from God the throne at his right hand because of what he endured. Rather, he has held the royal dignity throughout his existence. He is seated alongside the Father as God and wisdom and power, as we have said. He shares the Father's reign and is the creator of all things for the sake of the Father. He suffers no diminution in his divine dignity and knows the one who begot him just as he is known by his begetter. In short, recall the words of the Gospels: "No one knows the Son except the Father, and no one knows the Father except the Son" (Matthew 11:27; cf. John 10:15).

8   Do not separate the Son from the Father, or construct a compound and believe in a Son-Father. Believe rather that the one God has one only-begotten Son, who before all ages is God the Word, not an uttered word which is dispersed in the air, or like insubstantial words, but God the Son, the maker of rational beings, the Word who hears his Father and speaks himself. In due time, God willing, we shall explain this to you more fully, for we have not forgotten our intention of providing you now with a summary introduction to the creed.

On the Holy Spirit

16   Believe also in the Holy Spirit, and understand him correctly, for there are many who are at variance with the Holy Spirit and teach blasphemous doctrines about him. You have to learn that the Holy Spirit is one, indivisible, and endowed with many powers. His operations are many, but he himself is undivided. He knows the mysteries, and he "searches all things" (1 Corinthians 2:10), even the depths of God. He came down on the Lord Jesus Christ in the form of a dove. He worked through the law and the prophets. Now he will seal your soul at the time of baptism. Every rational nature needs the holiness that comes from him. If anyone presumes to blaspheme against him, he will not be forgiven either in this life or in the life to come (cf. Matthew 12:32). He receives the honor due to his rank together with the Father and the Son. Thrones and dominations, principalities and powers have need of him. For there is one God, the Father of Christ, and one Lord Jesus Christ, the only-begotten Son of the only God, and one Holy Spirit, who sanctifies and deifies all, who has spoken through the law and the prophets, the Old Testament and the New.

17   So keep always in your mind the seal of which we have now spoken to you summarily, touching on the most important points. However, if the Lord allows it, I shall speak about this later as best I can and give scriptural proof. For where the divine and holy mysteries of the creed are concerned, one must not teach even minor points without reference to the sacred Scriptures or be led astray lightly by persuasive and elaborate arguments. Do not simply take my word when I tell you these things unless you are given proof for my teaching from the holy Scripture. This is the guarantee of our creed: It is not merely a clever argument, but it is proved based on Scripture.

One can see Cyril's pastoral concern for his newest members through his teaching on the Holy Spirit and, previously, on Christ. He realizes the false doctrines that they are likely to hear.

Excerpts from Cyril's Preaching to the Newly Baptized in the Week after Easter

Early church bishops spent each day of the week after Easter preaching on the meanings of those things which the newly baptized had just experienced. These sermons were called mystagogy, since they led the neophytes into the "mysteries" of baptism and Communion. (Mystagogy comes from two Greek words that mean "lead" and "mysteries.") In these sermons, Cyril's concern, like that of other early bishops, was to name the different ways in which the various ceremonies had connected the newly baptized to the biblical story. Cyril preached these sermons from the mouth of Christ's tomb.

Careful readers might note that Cyril's description of Jerusalem does not always match perfectly with the other historical records like Egeria's diary or the anaphora of St. James. Why? Perhaps they come from different times and thus show different stages of development. Or perhaps Cyril's purpose in preaching made him focus on certain aspects without mentioning other details. Some even question whether the materials most scholars attribute to Cyril actually come from a different preacher, either earlier or later. Most scholars, however, do attribute these sermons to Cyril. Regardless, from our vantage point over a millennium and a half later, they still reflect the practice in Jerusalem in the fourth century, even if they do not coincide precisely with Egeria's diary.

Excerpts from several of Cyril's sermons are provided below. The numbering at the beginning of paragraphs reflects the scholarly practice of identifying different parts of a historic piece. Some numbers are skipped because only excerpts of the sermons are provided.

Mystagogic Catechesis 1: To the Newly Baptized

Reading: 1 Peter 5:8-11:"Be sober and wakeful . . ."

What God has done in Christ is the culmination of all that has come before. Note how Cyril speaks of Old Testament episodes as the "symbols" of the reality of salvation experienced in baptism.

Cyril is reinforcing the meaning of the renunciations which the baptismal candidates spoke at their baptism. Not only did they pledge faith to Christ at the time of baptism; they had to break all connection to everything not of his kingdom.

3   I invite you now to turn your attention from the old to the new, from symbol to reality. There Moses was sent by God to Egypt; here Christ is sent from the Father into the world. There Moses was to lead his oppressed people out of Egypt, and here Christ is sent to rescue his people in the world who are afflicted by sin. There the blood of the lamb warded off the destroyer; here the blood of the spotless Lamb Jesus Christ puts the demons to flight. Of old the tyrant pursued the people into the sea, but in your case this headstrong, shameless demon, who is the origin of all evil, followed you even into the springs of salvation. The earlier tyrant was drowned in the sea; here the tyrant disappears in the water of salvation.

4   Nonetheless you hear a voice telling you to stretch out your hand and say to him as if he were there before you: "I renounce you, Satan." I want to tell you why you stand facing west, for you need to know. The west is the region of visible darkness, and Satan is him-

self darkness and exerts his power in the dark. This is the meaning of the symbol of facing the west to renounce the prince of darkness and gloom. What then did you each stand and say? "I renounce you, Satan, you evil and savage tyrant," meaning: "I no longer fear your strength. For Christ has abolished it by allowing me to partake of his blood and his flesh, so as to destroy death by death through these his sufferings and to release me from perpetual slavery (cf. Hebrews 2:14-15). I renounce you, you subtle and crafty serpent. I renounce you, you schemer, who on the pretext of friendship introduced all wickedness and brought about the rebellion of our ancestors. I renounce you, Satan, author and partner in every evil."

5   Then you are told to pronounce a second phrase: "And all your works." Satan's works are every sin, which you must renounce, in the same way that someone who has escaped from a tyrant has escaped from his weapons as well. Every kind of sin is numbered among the devil's works. But I want you to realize that your words, especially at such an awe-inspiring moment as this, are inscribed in God's invisible records. So if ever you are caught doing something that contradicts your words, you will be judged a criminal. So renounce Satan's works, by which I mean all irrational actions and thoughts.

6   Then you say: "And all his pomp." These are the devil's pomp: a passion for the theatre, horse races, hunting, and all other such vain pursuits as those from which the saint begged God to free him when he said: "Turn away my eyes from beholding vanity" (Psalm 119:37). Do not indulge in a passion for the theatre, where the actors put on indecent spectacles full of every kind of shameless obscenity, and effeminate men perform wild dances. Do not share the passion of hunters, who expose themselves to wild beasts in order to indulge their wretched stomachs; to pamper their bellies with food, they become themselves food for the stomachs of savage beasts. To tell the truth, for the sake of their belly, which is their own god, they fight for their lives in single combat on the edge of a precipice. Avoid the races, a mad spectacle which unseats the soul. All these things are the devil's pomp.

The list of all Satan's pomp and worship gives a hint of how thoroughly Roman—not Jewish—the city of Aelia Capitolina (the Latin name for the city founded by Hadrian in the second century over the ruins of Jerusalem) had been.

8   Next you say: "And your worship." The devil's worship consists of prayers in the temples of idols, honors paid to lifeless idols, the lighting of lamps or burning of incense by springs and rivers. Some people have been tricked by dreams or demons into acting in this way, thinking they will even find a cure for bodily ailments, but you must have no part in such doings. Taking the auspices, divination, omens, amulets, writing on leaves, the use of charms or other spells — such things are the devil's worship. So avoid such actions, for if you give way to them after renouncing Satan and siding with Christ, you will find the tyrant will treat you more savagely. Perhaps he treated you before as one of his

family and spared you from some of the harshness of his service; but now that you have bitterly enraged him, not only will you lose Christ but you will learn what Satan is really like. You heard us telling you the story in the Old Testament about Lot and his daughters, didn't you? Wasn't he saved with his daughters when he reached the mountain, but his wife was turned into a pillar of salt, pilloried for all eternity to preserve the memory of the bad disposition she showed in looking back. Think of your own good, then, and once you have put your hand to the plow (cf. Luke 9:62), don't turn back to the bitter concerns of this life. Escape to the mountain, to Jesus Christ, to the stone cut without human hands which filled the world (cf. Daniel 2:34-45).

9   So when you renounce Satan and trample underfoot every contract you have made with him, you annul the old treaty made with hell, and there opens before you God's paradise which he planted in the east, and from which our ancestor was expelled because of his disobedience. You symbolize this by turning from the west to the east, which is the region of light. Then you are instructed to say: "I believe in the Father and in the Son and in the Holy Spirit and in one baptism of repentance." I spoke to you at length about these things in the earlier instructions according to the grace God gave me.

Mystagogic Catechesis 2: Concerning Baptism

Reading: Romans 6:3-14: "Do you not know that all of us who have been baptized into Christ Jesus have been baptized into his death? . . ."

4   After this you were led to the holy pool of sacred baptism, just as Christ was taken from the cross to the tomb which stands before you. Then you were each asked if you believed in the name of the Father and of the Son and of the Holy Spirit. You made the saving profession of faith, and three times you were immersed in the water and came up from it again. There in the font you symbolically re-enacted Christ's three-day burial. For just as our Savior spent three days and three nights in the heart of the earth, so too when you came up the first time you were imitating Christ's first day in the earth, and when you submerged, his first night. A man in the dark can no longer see, but during the day a man lives in the light; so too when you submerged, you could see nothing, as if it were night, but when you came up again, it was as if you were in daylight. At the same moment you both died and were born; that saving water became your tomb but also your mother. So what Solomon said in another context could be adapted to you. For in his book he wrote: "There is a time for giving birth and a time for dying" (Ecclesiastes 3:2). But with you it is the other way round: there is a time for dying and a time for being born, and one and the same time produces both results: your birth coincided with your death.

5   What a strange and wonderful thing! We did not literally die, we were not literally buried, we did not literally rise again after being crucified. We experienced these things only in symbols and representations; but salvation we experienced literally. Christ was really crucified and really buried and literally rose again, and all of this he did for our sake, so that by sharing his sufferings in imitation, we might gain salvation in truth. What unmeasured love this showed for mankind! Christ received the nails in his pure hands and experienced pain, and grants me salvation through sharing his experience without the pain and the toil.

Mystagogic Catechesis 3: Concerning the Anointing with Chrism

Reading: 1 John 2.20-8: "And you have received the anointing from God and know everything . . ."

1   Now that you have been baptized and have put on Christ, you have been shaped to the likeness of the Son of God. For when God predestined us for adoption, he shaped us to the likeness of Christ's glorious body. So now that you have shared in Christ, you are correctly called "christs" (anointed ones), so that God's words "Do not touch my christs" applies to you (Psalm 105:15). You have become christs now that you have received the sacramental sign of the Holy Spirit. Since you are images of Christ, everything which was done to you has a symbolic meaning.

When Christ had washed in the River Jordan and shared the touch of his divinity with the waters, he came up from them, and the Holy Spirit descended on him in substantial form, like resting upon like. So too when you came up from the holy waters of the font, your anointing took place, the sacramental sign of the anointing which Christ received. This anointing is the Holy Spirit, concerning whom blessed Isaiah spoke in the person of Christ in his prophecy concerning him: "The Holy Spirit has come upon me; that is why he has anointed me and sent me to announce the good news to the poor" (Isaiah 61:1).

4   First you are anointed on the forehead so as to be released from the shame which the first sinner carried around everywhere, and to reflect the glory of the Lord with face unveiled (cf. Exodus 34:29; 2 Corinthians 3:18). Next you are anointed on the ears so as to be given the ears spoken of by Isaiah (50:4): "And the Lord has given me an ear to hear," and by the Lord in the Gospels: "He that has ears to hear, let him hear" (Matthew 11:15). Next you are anointed on the nostrils, so that you may say, if you retain the sacred muron: "We are Christ's sweet fragrance before God among those who are saved" (2 Corinthians 2:15). After this you are anointed on your breast, so that you may "put on the breastplate of righteousness," and stand firm against "the devil's wiles" (Ephesians 6:14, 11). For just as the Savior went out and defeated his adversary after his baptism and the descent of the Holy

Cyril's sacramental theology is found in this paragraph. For him, the sacraments are not empty symbols. Although the newly baptized did not literally experience the events in the life of Christ to which baptism points, they did truly (literally) gain the salvation produced by those events.

Like other ancient preachers, Cyril's predilection is to find the terms for a present experience of salvation in the Scriptures themselves. Time and again he speaks of different ways the candidates have experienced the Gospel in the scriptural story. The sacrament incorporates (literally, embodies) God's mighty acts of salvation as witnessed in Scripture.

Spirit, so too, once you have been baptized and received the mystical anointing and put on the armor of the Holy Spirit, you have to stand against the power ranged against you and defeat it. For you can say: "I can do all things in Christ who empowers me" (Philippians 4:13).

In the Old Testament stories of Aaron and Solomon, Cyril finds the biblical examples (called types) that explain the significance of the anointing received in baptism in his church. They make new Christians into a royal priesthood. Note that Cyril prefers this sort of story-based explanation for the meaning of sacraments rather than abstractions.

6   You must understand that the symbolic explanation of this anointing with chrism is to be found in the Old Testament. For when Moses passed God's command on to his brother and installed him as high priest, he first made him bathe and then anointed him. Thus he was called the "christ"—a word derived from the anointing. So too, when the high priest made Solomon king, he anointed him after making him bathe in the Gihon (1 Kings 1:38-39). These rites were performed for them as a prefiguration, but for you not as a prefiguration but in reality, because your salvation began with the one who was anointed in reality by the Holy Spirit. For he is truly the firstfruits and you are the whole lump (cf. Romans 11:16); if the firstfruits are holy, it is clear that the holiness will spread to the whole lump.

Mystagogic Catechesis 4: Concerning Christ's Body and Blood

Reading: 1 Corinthians 11:23ff.: "For I received from the Lord the account which I passed on to you . . ."

Cyril is clear about what it is that Christians receive at the Lord's Supper: it is Christ's body and blood. He bases this explanation on an emphasis upon the Holy Spirit's work at Communion, among other things. He does not, however, use the term "transubstantiation," which is a Western term and another half millennium away from being coined.

3   So we receive with full assurance that what we are receiving is a share in Christ's body and blood. For in the form of bread you are given his body, and in the form of wine you are given his blood, so that by partaking of Christ's body and blood you may become of one body and one blood with Christ. In this way we become Christ-bearers, as his body and blood are spread around our limbs. Thus we become in blessed Peter's words "sharers of his divine nature" (cf. 2 Peter 1:4).

4   In an address to the Jews Christ once said: "Unless you eat my flesh and drink my blood, you do not have life within you" (John 6:53). Failing to understand the spiritual meaning of his words, they were scandalized and departed, believing that the Savior was urging them to cannibalism.

5   In the Old Testament there were "Loaves of the Presence" (Exodus 25:30; Leviticus 24:5-9; 1 Samuel 21:2-6), but as they belonged to the Old Testament, they came to an end. In the New Testament there is the bread of heaven and the cup of salvation, which sanctify both body and soul. Just as the bread is suitable for the body, so the Word is adapted to the soul.

6   So do not regard them as ordinary bread and wine, for they are the body and blood ac-
    cording to the Lord's declaration. For though your senses suggest this to you, let your
    faith reassure you. Do not judge by the taste, but draw from your faith unhesitating confi-
    dence that you have been granted Christ's body and blood.

Mystagogic Catechesis 5

Reading: 1 Peter 2:1ff.: "Therefore setting aside all evil and guile and slander . . ."

1   By God's goodness you have heard in the previous meetings all you needed to know about
    baptism, the anointing with chrism, and the partaking of Christ's body and blood. Now
    I must move on to what comes next, and today I shall set the coping-stone that is needed
    on the spiritual building.

2   So you saw the deacon giving water for washing to the bishop and to the presbyters stand-
    ing round God's altar. Of course, the deacon wasn't doing this because of any dirt on their
    bodies; that was not the reason. We didn't enter the church with dirt on our bodies in the
    first place. The washing was a symbol of our need to be cleansed of all our sins and trans-
    gressions. Since our hands stand for our actions, in washing them we are clearly symbol-
    izing purity and blamelessness of action. Surely you heard blessed David's explanation of
    this rite: "I shall wash my hands among the innocent, and walk around your altar, Lord"
    (Psalm 26:6). So to wash one's hands means not to be guilty of any sins.

3   Then the deacon calls out: "Greet one another; let us kiss one another." Don't take this kiss
    to be like the kiss friends exchange when they meet in the marketplace. This is something
    different; this kiss expresses a union of souls and is a plea for complete reconciliation. The
    kiss, then, is a sign that our souls are united and all grudges banished. This is what our Lord
    meant when he said: "If you are offering your gift on the altar and remember there that your
    brother has a complaint against you, leave your gift on the altar and go first and be recon-
    ciled with your brother, and then come and offer your gift" (Matthew 5:23-24). Thus the kiss
    is reconciliation, and so is holy, as blessed Paul implied when he proclaimed: "Greet one
    another with a holy kiss"; and Peter: "Greet one another with the kiss of charity."

Cyril is recalling part of the liturgy which they would have heard for the first time. What does he include, and what does he omit? These questions bedevil liturgical historians seeking to compare such descriptions with liturgical texts.

4   After this the bishop calls out: "Lift up your hearts." For indeed at this most awesome
    hour we ought to hold our hearts up to God and not keep them down below, involved with
    the earth and earthly things. In effect, then, the bishop is telling you all at this moment to
    lay aside the cares of this life and domestic worries and hold your hearts up to the loving
    God in heaven.

Then you reply: "We hold them up to the Lord," acknowledging by these words that you accept the bishop's instruction. Let no one present be disposed to say with their lips: "We hold them up to the Lord," while in their thought keeping their minds involved with earthly cares. You should, then, keep God in mind at all times; but if human weakness makes this impossible, at least at this moment you should make this your ideal.

5   Then the bishop says: "Let us give thanks to the Lord." We should indeed thank him for calling us to so great a grace when we were unworthy, for reconciling us when we were his enemies, for granting us the privilege of receiving the "Spirit of adoption" (Romans 8:15). Then you say: "It is worthy and just." For when we give thanks we perform a worthy and just action; but our Benefactor did not do what was just but what was more than just when he chose us to receive such great favors.

This is one of the few places where Cyril speaks about the musical experience of worship as he describes what people heard as they received Communion. He mentions one of his favorite themes: having faith so as to be able to discern more deeply than what one's senses perceive. Just as the danger in looking at Christ is to fail to see who he really is, so the danger in partaking of the elements is to fail to discern the deeper dimensions of Communion.

20   After this you hear the cantor to a sacred melody encouraging you to receive the holy mysteries. "Taste and see," he sings, "the goodness of the Lord" (Psalm 34:8). Do not rely on the judgment of your physical throat but on that of unhesitating faith. For what you taste is not bread and wine but Christ's body and blood, which they symbolize.

21   So when you approach, do not come with your wrists extended or your fingers parted. Make your left hand a throne for your right, which is about to receive the King, and receive Christ's body in the hollow of your hand, replying "Amen." Before you consume it, carefully bless your eyes with the touch of the holy body, watching not to lose any part of it; for if you do lose any of it, it is as if it were part of your own body that is being lost. Tell me, if someone gave you some golden filings, wouldn't you keep them safe and take care not to incur a loss through mislaying any of them? So shouldn't you take much greater care not to drop any crumbs of what is more precious than gold or gems?

22   Then, after receiving Christ's body, approach the cup of his blood. Do not stretch out your hands; bow down, say "Amen" as a form of worship or adoration, and sanctify yourself by partaking of Christ's blood. While your lips are still moist, touch them lightly with your hands and bless your eyes, your forehead, and your other senses. Then, as you wait for the prayer, thank God for admitting you to these great mysteries.

Source: The various homiletical materials from Cyril in this section come from Edward Yarnold's translations in *Cyril of Jerusalem* (New York: Routledge, 2000). Yarnold translated Cyril's sermon on the paralytic from *S. Patris Nostri Cyrilli Hierosolymorum Archiepiscopi Opera quae supersunt Omnia,* ed. W. K. Reischl and J. Rupp (Munich, 1848-60). The Lenten catechesis also came from this source. Yarnold translated the post-biblical mystagogical sermons from the critical edition published by A. Piedagnel as *Mystagogic Catecheses* SC 126 bis (Paris, 1988). As with many ancient texts, the question of authorship of patristic sermons sometimes is debated among scholars where the evidence is not absolutely clear. Some researchers, for example, have questioned whether Cyril was the preacher of the mystagogical sermons presented below (see the sermon excerpts in this section). For a defense of Cyril's authorship, see Alexis James Doval, *Cyril of Jerusalem, Mystagogue: The Authorship of the Mystagogic Catecheses* (Washington, D.C.: Catholic University of America Press, 2001). Doval's position is accepted widely. For a questioning of Cyril's authorship, see Juliette Day, *The Baptismal Liturgy of Jerusalem: Fourth- and Fifth- Century Evidence from Palestine, Syria, and Egypt* (Aldershot: Ashgate, 2007). The publication of Bishop Macarius's discussion of Jerusalem liturgy in 335 would call into question some of Day's conclusions. See Macarius of Jerusalem: *Letter to the Armenians, A.D. 335,* trans. Abraham Terian (Crestwood, N.Y.: St. Vladimir's Seminary Press; St. Nersess Armenian Seminary, 2008). For a different English translation of some of Cyril's sermons, see Lawrence J. Johnson's *Worship in the Early Church: An Anthology of Historical Sources,* vol. 2 (Collegeville, Minn.: Liturgical Press, 2010).

PART THREE

ASSISTING THE INVESTIGATION

Why Study Jerusalem's Worship?
Suggestions for Devotional Use

The following are suggestions for devotional use that correspond with specific sections of the book.

Describing Jerusalem's Worship

- Recall experiences of visiting places that are important to your family's history; perhaps these are childhood vacation spots, grandparents' farms, or even cemeteries. In what ways does returning to these places make you feel closer to your history or help you understand family stories better? Imagine what it might have been like to "walk where Jesus walked" only a short time after he walked there. How would standing in these places affect your experience of hearing God's stories? How would it make you feel closer to this part of your history?

- Christians in Jerusalem worshiped in various places in and around the city. Have you experienced worship as a physical journey? If so, reflect on your experiences of changing spaces as you worship. If not, consider reading some of the passages from the lectionary in this volume as you intentionally walk around your community. How does worshiping in different spaces affect your ideas of sacred space? Do you experience texts differently in different spaces?

- In reflecting on roles in worship, pp. 24-29 describe the bishop as the primary worship leader whose main responsibilities include administering Word and sacrament. What are your experiences with these two aspects of worship? How are they related? How prominent are they in your worship practices? Who administers them?

- The last few pages of this section describe the daily, weekly, and yearly rhythms of worship in Jerusalem. Draw a map of your daily, weekly, and/or yearly rhythms. Does your worship follow a pattern? How much variety do you experience in emotion? Are there parts of the pattern that comfort, affirm, and challenge your faith?

- This section closes with the words "They loved the Story and were moved by it." When have you most been moved by the Story? What about the Story most moves you?

People and Artifacts

- The image on p. 31 shows a posture of prayer. What words and emotions do you feel would be best expressed in this posture? What other postures do you commonly use in prayer?

Worship Setting and Space

- As you page through these depictions of Jerusalem's main worship space, observe the grandeur of the space. Imagine a throng wailing as they listened to the Gospel reading from the entrance to Christ's tomb. Picture yourself in this space as it was teeming with people who were translating to each other. What do you see? What do you hear? What do you smell? What do you feel? Where and how do you feel God in this space?

A Description of Worship

- After reading Egeria's account, write a journal entry describing worshiping experiences in your community from the perspective of a visitor. What details would you hope an observer would include? Are there details you would hope an observer would exclude? Why?
- Several places in Egeria's account describe a sensitivity toward hospitality in worship. What hospitable choices does Egeria highlight? What does your worshiping community do to enable the full, conscious, and active participation of all worshipers? What specific things could you do to provide more opportunity for this type of participation?

The Scripture Readings Likely Used in Jerusalem

- Choose a selection of days from various times throughout the year. Begin by reading the Psalm text. What emotion is expressed in the psalm? Put your body in a posture that reflects the tone of the psalm and read the texts for the occasion. How does your posture affect how you hear or read the texts?
- Carefully read the texts listed as the Vigil (group 44). Summarize each one in terms of God's activity.

The Communion Prayer Likely Used in Jerusalem

- Pray the prayer, especially the first two pages. Notice the Trinitarian nature of God. What are the names used for God? How is God described? Do you regularly recognize these attributes and actions of God in your prayer life? How does including them affect your mental image of who God is?

- Read through the rubrics. Observe the physical postures listed. Walk through the postures, holding each for five to ten seconds, and reflect on how your physical posture reflects the posture of the soul.

The Liturgy of St. James

- Pray the prayer of intercession that begins at the bottom of p. 105. After each "Let us pray to the Lord," pause for a time of silence and add prayer requests specific to your time and place before continuing to the next section.
- As you read through the liturgy, take note of aspects that might contribute to a sense of mystery. Do you experience mystery in worship? If so, in what ways? How might experiencing some of the more mysterious aspects of the liturgy change or challenge your experience of communion?

Sermons

- Consider the sermon Cyril preached to baptismal candidates at the beginning of Lent. What does he emphasize as key parts of Christian formation in the preparation for baptism? What, if any, advice does he give that would inform or support current approaches to discipleship?
- How does Cyril describe God? What sparks his passion for God?
- According to Cyril, what happens in baptism? Recall your baptism. In what ways do you daily live in your baptismal identity? List specific practices in your personal life or corporate worship experiences or brainstorm additional ones that remind you of your baptismal identity.

Why Study Jerusalem's Worship? Discussion Questions for Small Groups

The following are discussion questions for each section of this book.

General Introduction and Timeline

- What makes Jerusalem unique for the development of Christianity?
- What surprised you about Jerusalem from the time of Christ to the fourth century? Why?

Describing the Community's Worship

- Imagine what it might have been like to be a pilgrim to the Holy Land. What might motivate such a pilgrimage? Are there any similar practices we have?
- Christians moved from place to place around Jerusalem as they worshiped. How would this approach change our sense of worship space? How would this approach change our current sense of "belonging" to a particular church? What would be gained or lost?
- In your opinion, is our worship similar to the worship that Egeria experienced? In what ways? What can we learn from fourth-century Jerusalem about worshiping?

People and Artifacts

- The first illustration in this section shows a common posture for prayer. What emotion does this posture demonstrate? What does this posture communicate about the relationship between the person praying and God? Have you seen people take this posture in worship? Have you seen people take this posture in prayer? What postures do we use for prayer? What postures don't we use? What does this communicate about our relationship with God?
- Notice the connection between politics and worship. In what ways do politics affect our worship? Is this good, bad, or unavoidable?
- Is it surprising that nuns and monks played such an important role in the fourth-century church? How might ancient nuns provide an encouraging example to women today? And how could the monks give an example to men?

Worship Setting and Space

- As you look through these images, do you think these spaces give a greater sense of God being present among the people or of God being a distant, majestic ruler? What features contribute to either sense?
- Do you think the Jerusalem church gave too much emphasis to space and buildings? Why or why not?

A Description of Worship

- Note the times that Egeria describes people's emotions. What kinds of emotions occur during worship? What motivates these emotions? Do we and should we respond in our worship as they did?
- Egeria takes great effort to describe the rhythms of worship, especially yearly feasts and seasons. How many of these feasts and seasons does your church celebrate?
- In 31.3-4 Egeria mentions the accommodations made to enable both old and young to participate. What does this passage and other similar passages (such as 47.4 on the topic of language translation) tell us about the value that this worshiping community placed on participation and hospitality? Is there anything to be learned from this example?
- Several times Egeria comments on how readings or songs are "appropriate to the day or place." Why might this be significant? What do you think would make a reading or a song "appropriate" for a particular time or place of worship?
- How does the role of the bishop and other clergy compare to the role of the worshiper? Why might specific roles be reserved for specific people? What does this communicate about participation in worship?

The Scripture Readings Likely Used in Jerusalem

- Notice the number and variety of Scripture readings for specific services. Why might this be important? In what ways can the reading of Scripture be an act of worship?
- Look carefully at the instructions for those preparing to receive baptism (group 17). What does the selection of these particular passages tell you about what is important for new converts to know about their faith?
- Examine the readings listed in group 44. How would hearing these stories of God's salvation hours before Easter morning affect how you would hear the Easter resurrection story?

The Communion Prayer Likely Used in Jerusalem

- As you read through this communion prayer, notice the references to God, particularly the different persons of the Trinity. What do these tell you about how this worshiping community thinks about who God is and what God does?
- How does this communion prayer compare to the one used in your church?
- Can you imagine the content of this prayer being part of a sermon? What might this feature tell us about the relationship between praying and preaching?

The Liturgy of St. James

- In this service, how many different kinds of prayers are there? Is it possible to have too many prayers in worship? What kinds of things are prayed for? What do these requests tell us about how this community understands the relationship between God and God's people?
- This service seems very scripted. How does the Holy Spirit work through written texts? What is gained by using scripted texts? What is lost?
- At one point (p. 103), a deacon sends all the catechumens out of the service. Why might he do this? What does this communicate about what happens after their dismissal? Are there people we prevent from joining particular parts of our services? If so, why? What does this communicate about those parts of the service?

Sermons

- In Cyril's sermon on the paralytic by the pool, how does he describe who Jesus is? How important is it for Cyril to understand Jesus as the Incarnate God?
- Look through Cyril's Prologue to the Catecheses and his sermons to those preparing to be baptized. In Cyril's mind, what is the importance of baptism?
- The sermons for those preparing for baptism also demonstrate discipleship. What does Cyril focus on for those who are new to the faith? What are the main issues of belief, and what does he present as the greatest temptations? Would you point out the same topics now to those new to faith? If not, what would you change and why?

Why Study Jerusalem's Worship?
A Guide for Different Disciplines
and Areas of Interest

Christianity

If you are interested in Christianity as a religion generally, then Jerusalem is helpful for understanding the following:

- the rise of conscious Trinitarian definition and seeing how the period's theological discussions parallel developments in worship and vice versa;
- Christian emphasis upon the activity — not just the being — of God, particularly as seen in Jesus Christ;
- the era's relative shift in emphasis from looking ahead to the return of Christ to looking back at historical events;
- the impact that legalization of Christianity in the fourth century and the emperor's support had on the church.

Here are discussion questions based on these general religious issues:

- Should theological reflection precede changes in worship, or is it acceptable for liturgical practices to shape the belief system of a people?
- What are the multiple ways in which Jerusalem's worship reinforced an emphasis on the activity of God within time and space? Was Jerusalem creating something new in the pilgrims who flocked there, or was Jerusalem picking up on something already latent among Christians?
- Do you think Jerusalem's worship is in continuity with the early Christian emphasis upon the return of Christ as the basis for human hope?
- Did the emperor's support enhance the mission of the church in Jerusalem? Does a close relationship between church and government create impossible pitfalls or dangers?

Christian Worship

If you are interested in worship generally, then Jerusalem is helpful for understanding the following:

- how the Christian calendar developed with its yearly celebrations of events in the life of Christ;
- how Scripture—read, preached, and used in prayer—can provide the main content for worship;
- what a strong biblical spirituality in worship can look like;
- the importance of prayer (lots of it and lots of different kinds) in worship.

Here are discussion questions based on these general worship issues:

- Does the calendar of your church cover the major episodes in the life of Jesus Christ over a year, or does it focus on other things? How important is commemoration in Christian worship?
- Should a church have multiple Bible readings in a worship service? Why or why not?
- Why do you think the worshipers in Jerusalem were so moved when they heard the Bible read and preached?
- How much time should a church spend in praying during a worship service? What kinds of prayers are appropriate?

Evangelism and Discipleship

If you are interested in evangelism and discipleship, then Jerusalem is helpful for understanding the following:

- how making and initiating new Christians can be linked to the various aspects of a church's worship life;
- the role that a solid grounding in the Bible as a whole and in key Christian doctrines can have in preparing people for baptism.

Here are discussion questions based on these evangelism and discipleship issues:

- Was it helpful for the Jerusalem church to make baptizing and instructing new Christians such an important part of its public worship life?
- What should candidates for baptism be able to know and do before they are baptized? Is it useful to instruct them in key doctrines and help them to see how to hold the whole Bible together?

Spirituality

If you are interested in spirituality, then Jerusalem is helpful for understanding the following:

- the growing attachment early Christians had to sacred spaces;
- the rise of pilgrimage as a part of Christian devotion;
- the development of early monasticism.

Here are discussion questions based on these spirituality issues:

- For a Christian, what makes a space sacred? If heaven is our true home, should Christians be attached to special places?
- Can you empathize with early pilgrims' desire to get to Jerusalem even with the difficulty and cost of traveling in the fourth century?
- Is it a helpful thing to have people within the church — like monks and nuns — who dedicate their lives primarily to worship and prayer? What do "ordinary" Christians contribute to the church?

Preaching

If you are interested in preaching, then Jerusalem is helpful for understanding the following:

- how early preachers made Christ and his Gospel the key to interpreting all of Scripture;
- sermons which integrate relevance to the people, deep theology, and attentiveness to the Bible;
- a Trinitarian framework for understanding the Christian message of salvation.

Here are discussion questions based on these preaching issues:

- According to the examples in this book, how did an early preacher make Christ the linchpin of every sermon? Are current preachers as likely to use Christ as the key to interpreting the Old Testament or sacraments?
- Can relevance, theology, and Scripture be integrated in sermons today? Can modern preachers replicate what fourth-century preachers did? Why or why not?
- Even though Cyril's sermons are addressed to people and the prayer texts in the Liturgy of St. James are addressed to God, both speak about all three persons of the Trinity acting together for salvation. Why might they have this in common?

Glossary

Anaphora   Another term for the consecration prayer of Communion.

Anastasis   The name for Jerusalem's worship space around the tomb of Christ. The term means "resurrection" in Greek.

Antiphon   A word that literally means "voices against each other." It refers to the sung response (refrain) within a musical text. For instance, the main singer may sing the text, and the congregation may respond with the antiphon. The main thing to remember is that the word refers to a musical text being broken up and sung by two different singers/ groups.

Apotactite   A word that for Egeria appears to be synonymous with *monk* or *nun.* The term literally means "those set apart" — that is, those set apart from the world by renunciation of worldly goods.

Arianism   A major heresy named after its author, Arius, which denied the full divinity of Christ by claiming that the Son was created by the Father before the creation of the world. At the First Council of Nicea called by Emperor Constantine in 325, the church, with the leadership of Athanasius, condemned Arianism and declared the Father and the Son co-eternal, equal, and famously of the same substance, or "homoousios."

Atrium   The central court or open area at the entrance to a basilica.

Basilica   An early Christian church designed after the Roman halls of justice. Often a basilica has parallel aisles separated by rows of columns, which end in the apse, a semicircular structure with a raised platform.

Bishop   The highest order of ministry in the church. In the early church, bishops had responsibilities for teaching and preaching in worship, praying the key prayers in the administration of sacraments, overseeing the general health of a church and its outward ministries, and ordaining others to various orders of ministry.

Catechumen   Someone in preparation for baptism.

Diocese   The region under the administrative direction of a bishop. Within a diocese, the bishop is the chief ecclesiastical figure. After the legalization of Christianity, dioceses often followed the boundaries of the subprovincial civil administration districts of the Roman Empire.

Edicule   The architectural structure that surrounded the tomb of Christ after it had been freed from its original hillside setting.

Eleona   The basilica-type worship space atop the Mount of Olives.

Encaenia   The feast in September commemorating the dedication of Constantine's liturgical buildings.

Epiphany   The feast in Eastern Christianity on January 6. In Jerusalem, the commemoration was of the birth of Christ and the visitation of the Magi as recorded in Matthew 2.

Great Week   The week preceding Easter, filled with special worship services every day which commemorated the last week of Christ's life.

Heortae   The time of instruction, fasting, and other ascetic practices to prepare for worship around Easter. In Jerusalem it was the time for intensive preparation of those preparing for baptism on Easter. According to Egeria, it lasted eight weeks. Other regions called this season Lent.

Holy Sepulcher   The complex of worship spaces built on and around the sites of Christ's crucifixion and resurrection. The central worship site in Jerusalem, it consisted of the Martyrium, the Anastasis, and various spaces associated with the Cross or Golgotha.

Imbomon   The site on the Mount of Olives outside Jerusalem where Jesus was considered to have ascended to heaven.

Lazarium   The worship space built next to the tomb of Lazarus in Bethany, east of Jerusalem. It was the site of a stational liturgy nine days before Easter. (See John 11.)

Lucernare   A word derived from the Latin *lux* ("light") to describe an evening prayer service, so named because the lighting of lamps was an important ritual in the service. Egeria used a Western (Latin) word for the service, which would have had a Greek name in Jerusalem.

Martyrium   The basilica-type worship space built next to the site of Christ's crucifixion. As part of the Holy Sepulcher complex, the Martyium was one of the most important and most-used worship spaces in the city.

Mystagogy   A kind of specialized preaching that explores the meaning of the sacraments, particularly with reference to biblical stories. The Jerusalem church, like many ancient churches, spent the week after baptism preaching to the newly baptized, explaining how their liturgical experiences were actually experiences of the Gospel. In Greek, the term has the notion of leading someone into the "mysteries," i.e., both the "mystery" of the Gospel (cf. Ephesians 3:5) and the "mysteries" (an alternative name for sacraments) of the sacraments.

Octave   The period of eight days starting with a major feast/holiday.

Office   As used in this context, this term refers to prayer services, normally held on a daily basis and without sermon or sacrament.

Pascha   An ancient term for the passing over of Jesus Christ from death to life; it also refers to the cluster of worship services that remembered his crucifixion and resurrection.

Patristic   A term referring to the first several centuries of church history. The word is derived from the Latin word for "fathers," which is what the major church leaders of the period are called.

Presbyter An order of ministry a step "below" that of bishop and considered derived from that of bishop. Traditionally, the presbyter in worship is responsible for preaching the word and praying the key prayers in the administration of sacraments. The term is roughly equivalent to both "priest" and "elder."

Sion The original meeting place of the post-Easter Christian community. A new, larger worship space was built there in the fourth century. The events of Pentecost were associated with it.

Stational liturgy A way of worship that utilizes different sites — that is, stations — coordinated with rhythms of time and remembrance. This kind of worship was practiced in a unique way in Jerusalem. In effect, the whole city formed a single congregation that migrated from worship space to worship space.

Synaxis (plural: **synaxes**) An assembly for liturgical purposes.

Theotokos A theological name for the Virgin Mary which literally means "God-bearer." The term began to be used in the late patristic period as a way of affirming that Jesus Christ, whom she bore, was both truly man and truly God.

Trisagion A Greek word meaning "thrice holy," the "Holy, Holy, Holy" of Isaiah's vision (Isa. 6:3). It can also refer to the particular hymn of later liturgies: "Holy God, Holy Mighty, Holy Immortal, have mercy on us."

Suggestions for Further Study

Books and articles

Baldovin, John F. *Liturgy in Ancient Jerusalem*. Alcuin/GROW Liturgical Study 9 (Grove Liturgical Study 57). Cambridge: Grove Books, Ltd., 1989.

———. *The Urban Character of Christian Worship: The Origins, Development, and Meaning of Stational Liturgy*. Orientalia Christiana Analecta 228. Rome: Pont. Institutum Studiorum Orientalium, 1987.

Bradshaw, Paul F. "The Effects of the Coming of Christendom on Early Christian Worship." In *The Origins of Christendom in the West*. Edited by Alan Kreider. New York: T&T Clark, 2001.

———. *The Search for the Origins of Christian Worship: Sources and Methods for the Study of Early Liturgy*. New York: Oxford University Press, 2002.

Burreson, Kent J. "The Anaphora of the Mystagogical Catecheses of Cyril of Jerusalem." In *Essays on Early Eastern Eucharistic Prayers*. Edited by Paul F. Bradshaw. Collegeville, Minn.: Liturgical Press, 1997.

Day, Juliette. *The Baptismal Liturgy of Jerusalem: Fourth- and Fifth-Century Evidence from Palestine, Syria, and Egypt*. Liturgy, Worship, and Society Series. Aldershot and Burlington: Ashgate, 2007.

———. "Lent and the Catechetical Program in Mid-Fourth-Century Jerusalem." *Studia Liturgica* 35, no. 2 (2005): 129-47.

Doval, Alexis James. *Cyril of Jerusalem, Mystagogue: The Authorship of the Mystagogic Catecheses*. Washington: The Catholic University of America Press, 2001.

Walker, P.W.L. *Holy City, Holy Places: Christian Attitudes to Jerusalem and the Holy Land in the Fourth Century*. New York: Oxford University Press, 1990.

Wilken, Robert. *The Land Called Holy: Palestine in Christian History and Thought*. New Haven: Yale University Press, 1992.

Wilkinson, John. *Egeria's Travels*. London: SPCK, 1971; revised ed.: Warminster: Aris & Phillips, 2002.

Witvliet, John D. "The Anaphora of St. James." In *Essays on Early Eastern Eucharistic Prayers*. Edited by Paul F. Bradshaw. Collegeville, Minn.: Liturgical Press, 1997.

Yarnold, Edward. *Cyril of Jerusalem*. New York: Routledge, 2000.

Web sites

Photos and other information on the current state of the Holy Sepulcher can be found at

http://www.christusrex.org/www1/jhs/TSspmenu.html

For a virtual tour of the current Holy Sepulcher, go to

http://www.360tr.com/kudus/kiyamet_eng/index.html

For more extensive bibliographies on Egeria, see the links found at

http://www.hs-augsburg.de/˜Harsch/Chronologia/Lsposto4/Egeria/ege_intr.html

Works Cited

Aetheria. *On the Mysteries: With Three Hymns.* English translation by J.H. Bernard, 1891.

Armstrong, Karen. *Jerusalem: One City, Three Faiths.* New York: Alfred A. Knopf, 1996.

Avi-Yonah, Michael. *The Jews of Palestine.* Oxford: Blackwell, 1976.

Baldovin, John F. "A Lenten Sunday Lectionary in Fourth-Century Jerusalem." In *Time and Community: Studies in Liturgical History and Theology,* edited by J. Neil Alexander, pp. 115-22. Washington, D.C.: The Pastoral Press, 1990.

————. *Liturgy in Ancient Jerusalem.* Alcuin/GROW Liturgical Study 9 (Grove Liturgical Study 57). Cambridge: Grove Books, Ltd., 1989.

————. "Sunday Liturgy in Jerusalem: A Pilgrim'sView." In *Worship — City, Church, and Renewal.* Washington, D.C.: The Pastoral Press, 1991.

————. *The Urban Character of Christian Worship: The Origins, Development, and Meaning of Stational Liturgy.* Orientalia Christiana Analecta, 228. Rome: Pont. Institutum Studiorum Orientalium, 1987.

Biddle, Martin. *The Church of the Holy Sepulchre.* New York: Rizzoli, 2000.

Bradshaw, Paul F. "The Influence of Jerusalem on Christian Liturgy." In *Jerusalem: Its Sanctity and Centrality to Judaism, Christianity, and Islam,* edited by Lee I. Levine, pp. 251-59. New York: Continuum, 1999.

————. *The Search for the Origins of Christian Worship: Sources and Methods for the Study of Early Liturgy.* New York: Oxford University Press, 2002.

Brightman, F.E. *Liturgies Eastern and Western,* 1896.

Burnett, Jill S. "Congregational Song and Doctrinal Formation: The Role of Hymnody in the Arian/Nicene Controversy." *Liturgical Ministry* 10 (Spring 2001): 83-92.

Connell, Martin F. "Heresy and Heortology in the Early Church: Arianism and the Emergence of the Triduum." *Worship* 72, no. 2 (March 1998): 117-40.

Conybeare, F. C. *Rituale Armenorum,* 1896.

Corpus Christianorum, Series Latina, vol. 175. Turnhout, Belgium: Brepols, 1965.

Coüasnon, Charles. *The Church of the Holy Sepulchre in Jerusalem.* Translated by J.P.B. Ross and Claude Ross. Plates VIII, XVII. London: Oxford University Press for the British Academy, 1974.

Cuming, G.J. "Egyptian Elements in the Jerusalem Liturgy." *Journal of Theological Studies* 25, no. 1 (1974): 117-24.

Day, Juliette. *The Baptismal Liturgy of Jerusalem: Fourth- and Fifth-Century Evidence from Palestine, Syria, and Egypt.* Aldershot and Burlington: Ashgate, 2007.

Doval, Alexis James. *Cyril of Jerusalem, Mystagogue: The Authorship of the Mystagogic Catecheses.* Washington, D.C.: The Catholic University of America Press, 2001.

Fink, Peter, ed. *The New Dictionary of Sacramental Worship.* Collegeville, Minn.: Liturgical Press, 1990.

Hunt, E. D. *Holy Land Pilgrimage in the Later Roman Empire, A.D. 312-460.* New York: Oxford University Press, 1982.

Hutter, Irmgard. *Early Christian and Byzantine Art.* New York: Universe Books, 1988.

Irshai, Oded. "From Oblivion to Fame: The History of the Palestinian Church (135-303 C.E.)." In *Christians and Christianity in the Holy Land: From the Origins to the Latin Kingdoms,* edited by Ora Limor and Guy G. Stroumsa, pp. 91-140. Turnhout, Belgium: Brepols, 2006.

Jasper, Ronald Claud Dudley, and G.J. Cuming, translators. "Anaphora of St. James." In *Prayers of the Eucharist: Early and Reformed,* pp. 88-99. Collegeville, Minn.: Liturgical Press, 1990.

Johnson, Lawrence J. *Worship in the Early Church: An Anthology of Historical Sources.* 4 vols. Collegeville, Minn.: Liturgical Press, 2010.

Jungmann, Joseph A. *The Place of Christ in Liturgical Prayer.* Collegeville, Minn.: Liturgical Press, 1989.

MacMullen, Ramsay. *Christianity and Paganism in the Fourth to Eighth Centuries.* New Haven: Yale University Press, 1997.

Murphy-O'Connor, Jerome. "Pre-Constantinian Christian Jerusalem." In *The Christian Heritage in the Holy Land,* edited by Anthony O'Mahony et al., pp. 13-21. London: Scorpion Cavendish, 1995.

Prinz, O. *Itinerarium Egeriae.* Heidelberg, 1960.

Reif, Stefan C. "The Early History of Jewish Worship." In *The Making of Jewish and Christian Worship,* edited by Paul F. Bradshaw and Lawrence A. Hoffman, pp. 109-36. Notre Dame: University of Notre Dame Press, 1991.

Renoux, Athanase. "Le Codex Arménien Jérusalem 121." *Patrologia Orientalis* 36, no. 2 (1971): 210-373.

Roberts, Alexander, and James Donaldson, eds. *The Ante-Nicene Fathers: Translations of the Writings of the Fathers Down to A.D. 325.* Grand Rapids: Wm. B. Eerdmans, 1951.

Senn, Frank C. *Christian Liturgy: Catholic and Evangelical.* Minneapolis: Fortress Press, 1997.

Spinks, Bryan D. "The Jerusalem Liturgy of the *Catecheses Mystagogicae:* Syrian or Egyptian?" *Studia Liturgica* 18, no. 2 (1989): 391-95.

Stringer, Martin D. *A Sociological History of Christian Worship.* Cambridge: Cambridge University Press, 2005.

Talley, Thomas J. *The Origins of the Liturgical Year.* New York: Pueblo, 1986.

Terian, Abraham, translator. *Macarius of Jerusalem: Letter to the Armenians, A.D. 335.* Crestwood, N.Y.: St. Vladimir's Seminary Press, 2008.

Vretska, K. *Die Pilgerreise der Aetheria (Peregrinatio Aetheria)*. Klosterneuburg, 1958.

Wainright, Geoffrey, and Karen B. Westerfield Tucker, editors. *The Oxford History of Christian Worship*. New York: Oxford University Press, 2006.

Walker, Peter. "Jerusalem and the Holy Land in the Fourth Century." In *The Christian Heritage in the Holy Land,* edited by Anthony O'Mahony et al., pp. 22-34. London: Scorpion Cavendish, 1995.

————. "Pilgrimage in the Early Church." In *Explorations in a Christian Theology of Pilgrimage,* edited by Craig Bartholomew and Fred Hughes, pp. 150-52. Burlington: Ashgate, 2004.

Wilkinson, John. *Egeria's Travels*. London: SPCK, 1971. Revised edition: Warminster: Aris & Phillips, 1981.

Witvliet, John D. "The Anaphora of St. James." In *Essays on Early Eastern Eucharistic Prayers,* edited by Paul F. Bradshaw, pp. 153-72. Collegeville, Minn.: Liturgical Press, 1997.

Yarnold, Edward. *Cyril of Jerusalem*. New York: Routledge, 2000.

Index

159